THE ORIOLE BOOK

THE ORIOLE BOOK

Nancy Flood

STACKPOLE
BOOKS

Published by
STACKPOLE BOOKS
5067 Ritter Road
Mechanicsburg, PA 17055
www.stackpolebooks.com

Printed in China

10 9 8 7 6 5 4 3 2 1

Cover design by Caroline M. Stover
Cover photo by Brian E. Small
Photos on pages 17, 21, 30, 34, 58, 61, and 69 © Daybreak Imagery
Photos on pages 5, 12, and 74 © Maslowski Wildlife Productions
All artwork by Amelia Hansen

Library of Congress Cataloging-in-Publication Data

Flood, Nancy J. (Nancy Jean)
  The oriole book / Nancy Flood.
      p. cm.
  ISBN-13: 978-0-8117-3597-1
  ISBN-10: 0-8117-3597-4
  1. Icterus (Birds). I. Title.
  QL696.F2475F56 2009
  598.8'74—dc22

                                        2009016208

CONTENTS

1

What Is an Oriole?

To hear an Oriole sing
May be a common thing—
Or only a divine.

—EMILY DICKINSON

A flash of orange, a burst of whistled song, and a male Baltimore Oriole flies into a cottonwood tree on the edge of a creek. Landing beside his olive-colored mate, he watches while she works industriously, weaving a piece of grass back and forth until it is intertwined with the hundreds of other such pieces she has collected already. An amazing, baglike hanging structure takes shape—a safe nest in which she will lay and incubate her eggs and then, with her mate's help, feed her nestlings until they are ready to fly on their own. The family will then stay more or less together for another few weeks, until it is time to leave their summer home and travel south to where the winters are warm and the food abundant. Next spring, those that have survived a staggering array of hazards will return to repeat the cycle, once again filling the forests, gardens, and parks of the United States and Canada with their songs, calls, and colors.

This book is about orioles: especially Baltimore and Bullock's Orioles, but also Scott's and Orchard and Hooded Orioles and all of their close relatives—the twenty-eight or so species in the group of birds technically referred to as the genus *Icterus*—the New World Orioles. As their membership in a single genus would suggest, these species share certain features. In fact, research has shown that the genus *Icterus* is monophyletic, meaning that its members have all evolved from a single ancestral species.

1

In all New World orioles, for example, males (and often the females, too) have a more or less "typical" plumage type: they display some variation on a theme of black interspersed with orange or yellow plumage, with white markings, usually on the wings. All female orioles build nests that are more or less pendant—suspended from, rather than sitting on, the twigs or branches to which they are attached. As well, most orioles have melodious whistled songs that are often described as having a flutelike quality; they may also share an array of chattering calls. As far as we know, all members of the genus are monogamous, which means they have one mate at a time. Biparental care is another general characteristic: although only females build nests and incubate the eggs, both parents are involved in feeding and caring for the young.

The numerous great-great-grandchildren of a single couple can also be quite different, however, and so too are the orioles. Over evolutionary time, the many oriole species have experienced a diversity of selection pressures: varying physical environments and different competitors and predators, as well as chance events, have all had their effects. Thus, despite the fact that they share many features, orioles also vary in interesting ways. For example, although the species most familiar to us are migratory, most orioles are resident: they are found year-round within their range. And whereas these migratory species are sexually dimorphic (males and females look quite different), most of the resident forms are monomorphic: males and females are virtually indistinguishable in appearance.

And of course, although many species share the distinctive "oriole" appearance, this too varies. For example, the Epaulet Oriole's black plumage is relieved only by a dash of color at the leading edge of the wing and in its thigh feathers. In some populations (termed subspecies), this "epaulet" is yellow, as are the legs, whereas in others the epaulet is chestnut-colored and the legs black. At the opposite extreme is the Yellow Oriole. As its name suggests, it is predominantly yellow, with black wings, a black line running from the eyes to the beak, and a thin black bib. Although all orioles apparently replace their plumage once a year, during the process of molting, some (such as the Baltimore Oriole) do this while on the breeding grounds, while others wait until later in the year, during the nonbreeding season. The Orchard Oriole, for example, molts after it has arrived on its wintering grounds. Still others, such as the Bullock's Oriole, molt at stopover sites during their migratory journey.

These differences existing in such a closely related group of species have made the genus *Icterus* the subject of considerable study in recent years. As scientists have acquired new tools that allow them to scrutinize genes, they have been able to develop detailed hypotheses about the relationships among the various oriole species—which are closely and which are distantly related to each other, for example, and the ones that are probably most like the ancestor from which they all evolved. Thus, they can trace the evolutionary pathways along which changes in plumage, migratory status, sexual dimorphism, and other features have occurred. Examining these changes in the context of the environments in which the species live allows scientists to test hypotheses about the adaptive value (if any) of traits such as the timing of molt, the tendency to migrate, and the possession of sexual dimorphism.

"TRUE" ORIOLES

Some historical records suggest that the name "oriole" was apparently first used—in its Latin form, *oriolus*—in 1250 by Albertus Magnus, a Dominican friar well known for his comprehensive knowledge of science and advocacy of cooperation between science and religion. Of course, Magnus used the name to describe a species of bird living in the Old World—probably the Golden Oriole of Great Britain. One version of the story is that to him the word *oriolus* sounded much like the song of the bird he was describing. In 1758, Karl von Linne, the inventor of the two-part system for naming species (that is, the system of binomial nomenclature) gave the Golden Oriole the technical name *Oriolus oriolus.* Von Linne typically used Latin words for his names (he even latinized his own name, and today we also know him as Linnaeus) and liked them to have some meaning. To create the name for this bird, he took the Classical Latin word *aureolus,* meaning "golden." One way or another, either for its color or its song, this Eurasian species was the first to bear the name oriole.

Today, the name is still applied to the Golden Oriole and its close relatives: a family of medium-sized birds commonly called the "true" or "forest" orioles and given the technical family name Oriolidae. The family includes about thirty species of birds (grouped into two genera) that live in Africa, Europe, Asia, and Australia. Like our New World orioles, the males of these Old World species are commonly yellow with black on the wing, tail, and head and most have melodious songs as well as an array of harsher calls. Also, like our orioles, females of many species in the Oriolidae family weave hanging nests. Because of these similarities, the common name "oriole" also came to be applied to members of the genus *Icterus*, even though New World and Old World orioles are not at all related.

NEW WORLD ORIOLES

The New World orioles, which are found only in North, Central, and South America, comprise approximately twenty species that are closely enough related to be grouped together in one genus. The name *Icterus* comes from the ancient Greek word *ikteros* through the Latin word *ictericus*, which means "yellow" or "jaundiced one."

Nine of the *Icterus* orioles have been known to breed in North America, three of which, the Baltimore, Orchard, and Bullock's Orioles, commonly nest in the United States and parts of Canada. The first two of these three are generally found in the eastern and central portions of the continent, whereas the Bullock's Oriole is confined to the west. The other six *Icterus* orioles do not nest in Canada and can be thought of as Mexican birds that venture into the United States. Scott's and Hooded Orioles breed in the southwestern part of the country, while Altamira and Audubon's Orioles breed in the southern part of Texas. The Streak-backed Oriole is a casual visitor to the United States, mainly to the southern parts of Arizona and California in the fall and winter. However, because there are only three published records of Streak-backed Oriole nests in the United States—from southern Arizona in 1993 and 1994—it cannot yet be considered a true "North American" oriole. All five of these species commonly breed in Mexico. Finally, the Spot-breasted Oriole lives on the east coast of Florida, where it was introduced in the late 1940s, probably as a result of the escape of caged birds.

Mexico is really the center of distribution for the genus. Sixteen species breed primarily or only in this country. Eight are restricted to South America, while five are indigenous to the West Indies and have very limited ranges. The Greater Antillean Oriole is found only in Cuba, Hispaniola, Puerto Rico, the Bahamas, and other smaller islands in this area. The Jamaican Oriole is found only in Jamaica, and the St. Lucia, Martinique, and Montserrat Orioles are found only on the islands after which they are named.

In addition to the size of the range they occupy, the size of the birds themselves and their nests also varies within the genus. The smallest

A Baltimore Oriole in colorful breeding plumage is a welcome sight in spring throughout much of central and eastern North America. The species is the most common oriole in the United States and Canada.

oriole is the Orchard Oriole, which is 6 to 7 inches in total length and weighs 0.67 to 0.81 ounce. By comparison, the Baltimore Oriole is a middle-sized species at about 7 to 8 inches in length and 1.09 to 1.23 ounces in weight. The Altamira Oriole is one of the largest species in the genus, at 9 to almost 10 inches in length and a weight of 2.11 to 2.29 ounces. In most species, females are about 5 percent smaller than males—a relatively small amount of sexual size dimorphism compared with that characteristic of many types of birds.

Although the characteristic oriole nest is an intricately woven, hanging, baglike structure, the size and form of nests do vary among the species in this genus. The nests of Scott's Orioles are more cuplike than bag-shaped, although they are woven from plant fibres and hang from the leaves (usually of yucca and other similar plants) to which they are attached. Orchard Orioles have among the smallest nests of the genus. They are only as deep as they are wide—about 3 inches. By comparison, the hanging nests of Altamira Orioles can be 2 feet long and quite conspicuous; some females suspend them from power lines.

Three of the species of orioles found in South America are commonly referred to as troupials, specifically the Venezuelan, Orange-backed, and Campo troupial. Unique in several ways, troupials have yellow eyes (those of other orioles are dark) and an area of bare, blue-colored skin around these eyes. Their most "unoriolelike" characteristic is that they do not build their own nests. Rather they are known as nest pirates—they steal the fully or partially built nests of a selection of species that breed in the same area.

HOW MANY SPECIES?

You may have noticed that the number of species in the genus *Icterus* has not been given as an exact number. The reason for this is that the number varies. It actually depends on many factors—what recent discoveries have been made, who is in charge of defining and/or naming the species, what source you read, how old that source is, and so on.

Indeed, part of the issue depends on how the term "species" is defined. Although there is a variety of ways to do this, most scientists would define a species as a group of individuals that can potentially interbreed with each other to produce fertile offspring but which cannot breed with individuals from outside their own species' grouping. This definition works well when thinking about unrelated species—those that have followed separate evolutionary paths for a long time. Dogs and cats, for example, are quite clearly different species. Dogs and wolves, however, which are much more closely related, pose a problem for this definition. We used to think of each as separate species and for a long time had identified them as such. Linnaeus had given each its own technical name: *Canis lupus* for the wolf and *Canis familiaris* for the dog.

It is clear, though, that domesticated dogs evolved from wolves; they were, in fact, running with wolves in the not-too-distant past. Although generations of highly selective breeding by humans have produced some odd dog breeds that are quite different from wolves, many dogs are still quite wolflike. And we know that interbreeding between the two species happens relatively frequently, producing what is referred to as hybrid offspring. Horses and donkeys, which are separate species, also inter-breed, of course, producing a hybrid offspring known as a mule. Mules are sterile, however, which means that horses and donkeys do fit the defi-nition for species given above. In contrast, the hybrid offspring of dogs and wolves are typically quite fertile—so are these two taxa really differ-ent species? In 1993, after much consideration, the Smithsonian Institution and the American Society of Mammalogists decided that in fact they should not be recognized as separate and the domestic dog is now offi-cially designated as a subspecies of the wolf. Since subspecies are given three-part names that show their lineage, dogs are designated *Canus lupus familiaris.*

The same sort of issue exists for the New World orioles, all of which are closely related. Wherever the ranges of two oriole species overlap there is the potential for them to interbreed—and many of what are today referred to as separate species do, in fact, interbreed and produce fertile offspring. The Baltimore and Bullock's Orioles present a classic case of this—and of the problem of counting numbers of species. Although we cannot know for sure, these two might have once very long ago consti-tuted a single homogenous species. Individuals of this single form might have once lived throughout North America until climatic conditions isolated two populations of the form, each of which might have evolved separately in different environments.

Doubtless, the First Nations peoples who first lived in North America had their own names for the orioles they saw every day. The birds were given their first formal English names only after European explorers began traversing the New World, often taking or sending specimens back home to European museums and collectors. When the orioles we now know as the Baltimore and Bullock's were discovered and named (in 1731 and 1837, respectively—the west being explored later than the east) they differed somewhat in size and were quite different in appearance, behav-ior, timing of molt, and song.

People tend to change habitats, however, and as early as a thousand years ago, First Nations inhabitants of North America had begun farming and establishing villages along rivers in the Great Plains. The arrival of European settlers, "filling up" the east and then venturing west to become pioneers in new lands, accelerated this process. With farms and villages, then towns and cities, came trees. Planted for windbreaks, shade, and pleasure, trees filled once-treeless areas of the Great Plains, creating suitable breeding habitat for various types of birds, including orioles. No one knows when the first mixed pair of Baltimore and Bullock's Orioles threw caution to the wind and mated, but people began writing about it in the early part of the twentieth century and it was studied carefully in the 1950s by Charles Sibley and Lester Short, who collected orioles across Nebraska and Colorado. They described a zone about 150 to 200 miles wide in which hybridization was quite common. And not only was hybridization occurring, the hybrids were fertile. Sibley and Short thus concluded that the two birds were conspecific—members of the same species—and they published a paper to this effect in 1964.

In 1983, the Committee on Classification and Nomenclature, a standing committee of the American Ornithologist's Union (A.O.U.), agreed with this conclusion. The Baltimore and Bullock's Orioles were lumped together and renamed as a single species: the Northern Oriole. (Since the rules of naming species give precedence to the first specific epithet [the second half of the binomial designation] ever given, the technical name for this new species was *Icterus galbula,* which had been the moniker of the first-named Baltimore variety. The two species could still be referred to, but only as subspecies of the single new one; they were designated *Icterus galbula galbula* and *Icterus galbula bullockii.*)

For the next decade, all research papers, popular articles, or government reports written on either (or both) of these species referred to it (or them) as the Northern Oriole. Any new field guides, or new editions of old field guides, published during this time period also used this name.

Meanwhile, the hybrid zone continued to be the subject of much scrutiny. Scientist James Rising noted that although hybridization was certainly occurring, it did not appear to be increasing in frequency. That is, the zone was not getting any wider, and even in the middle of the area of hybridization, there were still a few birds that appeared to be pure Baltimore or Bullock's Orioles. (Partly because he had a slightly different view of what defined a species, Rising had recommended in 1970 that the two continue to be recognized as separate species.)

Eventually, the A.O.U. changed its mind. In a supplement to the checklist published in 1995, the Baltimore Oriole and Bullock's Oriole were once again given the status of separate species, with their familiar names intact. Recent research has, in fact, indicated that these two are not even each other's closest relatives. The Baltimore Oriole is more closely related to the Black-backed Oriole than it is to the Bullock's, and the Bullock's sister species seems to be the Streak-backed Oriole.

This is only one of several oriole stories that show why it is difficult to settle on the exact number of species that can be said to constitute the genus. The seventh edition of the A.O.U. checklist was published in 1998. Since then, the yearly considerations of the Classification and Nomenclature Committee, published as supplements in the official journal of the A.O.U., have added yet another species: In 2000, the Black-cowled Oriole (*Icterus prosthemelas*), which had been a subspecies of the Greater Antillean Oriole, was split out to become a species in its own right, making a total of twenty-three North and Central American *Icterus* species described in the checklist. In 2004 and 2008, the committee considered, but decided against, a proposal to split the Orchard Oriole into two species, the Orchard and Fuertes' Orioles. In 2006, it decided against a proposal to split the Greater Antillean Oriole even further, into as many as four separate species (living separately on different islands in the Greater Antilles group of islands, they seem to be different species to some observers). Currently, the list adds five species found only in South America to the 2000 list, bringing the total *Icterus* species number to twenty-eight. The actual number of species, however, seems to be a moving target (and this is perhaps as it should be, since evolution is an ongoing process).

ATYPICAL NORTHERNERS

Interestingly, the orioles that North Americans probably know best are actually rather atypical of the genus. For example, of the eight North American orioles, the three that breed in colder regions (in Canada as well as in the United States) are, not surprisingly, the most migratory species in the entire genus. On average, the Baltimore Oriole travels over thirty-five degrees of latitude between breeding and nonbreeding seasons, nesting as far north as the Peace region of British Columbia and wintering from southern Mexico through Central America to Venezuela and Colombia. The average Orchard Oriole, by comparison, moves over twenty-seven degrees of latitude. Its breeding range doesn't extend as far north as that of the Baltimore Oriole, and some individuals winter north of the Baltimore's winter range, along both coasts of Mexico. The Bullock's Oriole moves over twenty-three degrees of latitude. It breeds only in the very southern parts of Canada and winters mainly in Mexico and northern Central America.

Of the other oriole species, only two can really be considered regular migrants: the Hooded and Scott's Orioles both move over fourteen or so degrees of latitude on average, breeding mainly in the southern United

States and wintering in Mexico. The Black-backed Oriole (also known as the Abeille's Oriole) moves over four degrees of latitude, and the Fuertes', Streak-backed, and Black-vented Orioles move a short distance, about one degree of latitude, between breeding and nonbreeding seasons. All the rest of the orioles are considered residents. Staying put is thus the rule in the genus, which makes sense, since most species live in tropical or subtropical regions.

All of the truly migratory species are also strongly sexually dimorphic— again unlike most of the other orioles. In thirteen of the oriole species, males and females are virtually indistinguishable—at least to humans— and both sexes have brightly colored plumage. They are thus referred to as sexually monomorphic. This is the case for the two orioles that breed in South Texas, the Altamira and Audubon's Orioles, and the species that breeds in Florida, the Spot-breasted Oriole. The situation is quite different for the Baltimore, Bullock's, Orchard, Scott's, and Hooded Orioles, however. In these, males are brightly colored and females have a much duller, cryptic plumage, making the sexes easy to tell apart.

2

What Do Orioles Eat?

The foods that promote longevity, virtue,
strength, health, happiness, and joy are juicy, smooth,
substantial, and agreeable to the stomach.

—The Bhagavad Gita

All of our North American orioles, and probably most, if not all, of the other species in the genus *Icterus* eat a combination of insects, fruit, and nectar, as well as small amounts of other animals and material. The exact nature of the food items in these categories and the relative abundance of each vary with season, location, and species.

EATING INSECTS

Orioles favor insects in early spring, when few fruits or flowers are available. They are also the food of choice for parents feeding young because of their high protein content. Just as in humans, this nutrient is required for the production of muscle and other body tissues in growing nestlings. In one study of the Bullock's Oriole's eating habits, the contents of the stomachs of 162 California birds were analyzed. The remains consisted of 79 percent animal matter and 21 percent vegetable matter. Some 35 percent of the animal material consisted of beetles (most of these were the remains of beetle species that were injurious to crops in the area, such as weevils). Ants, bees, wasps, various types of scale insects, stinkbugs, leafhoppers, tree hoppers, and Lepidoptera (adult moths, pupae, and caterpillars) were also found in quantity.

Orioles eat a variety of insects whenever they are available. Fruit and nectar also make up a large part of their diet. Seeds, in general, are ignored.

In fact, orioles seem to take any insects they can, small or large. They do, however, seem to specialize to some extent on certain kinds of insects when and where they are most available. The Baltimore Oriole is well known for its fondness for the hairier sorts of caterpillars that many other birds generally avoid. It eats many of the caterpillars we love to hate, including fall webworm, the larvae of the gypsy moth, the tussock caterpillar, and the forest tent caterpillar, often tearing open the webs to extract the meal.

Other oriole species (and indeed some other songbirds) also eat tent caterpillars, but with less gusto, it appears. The Bullock's Oriole, for example, has been known to puncture the skin and withdraw the juicy material inside the caterpillar, dropping the hairy exoskeleton. Some actually seem to hit the caterpillar against a branch until the skin separates from the internal tissues. In addition to feasting on these particular pests, orioles are to be thanked for taking a wide variety of other injurious insects. Once the orioles discover how to locate and retrieve a particular kind of food, they continue to repeat the behavior until the supply is used up. They will work their bills into curled leaves over and over again to retrieve the leaf rollers inside or examine crevices in bark to find hidden coddling moth pupae. In 1924, an early Texas naturalist described how Orchard Orioles seemed to be one of the few species of bird that had learned to find boll weevils hiding in cotton plants. Other observers noted that Bullock's Orioles also had the same talent. In 1912, a writer noted that in Illinois, Orchard Orioles killed in an orchard infested with canker-worms were found to have their stomachs full of these caterpillars. Other authors of that era described Baltimore Orioles taking their newly fledged young to potato patches to feed on potato beetles. Today, in many places, pesticides have taken the place of birds as insect control agents in orchards and fields. There are still many insects out there, however, infesting our forests and gardens, and orioles clearly have the talent to find them.

Bullock's, Baltimore, and Orchard Orioles are often more comfortable foraging in trees, gleaning insects from bark, twigs, or leaves—although they will come down to the ground if a food bonanza awaits (in fact, some seem particularly fond of grasshoppers when they are available; in one area in California, Bullock's Orioles ate an average of forty-five grasshoppers a day). Others species, like the Scott's Oriole and Hooded Oriole, which live in more open, desert scrub country, usually pick up insects on the ground or in shrubs not far above it. They are thus even more likely to consume grasshoppers, crickets, and other ground-dwelling insects.

All oriole species have been observed poking into flowers, since these are often good places to find insects, as well as nectar. In addition, all orioles can also catch insects on the wing and do so when the situation warrants: adult butterflies and moths that have emerged from pupae that orioles have missed and are massing to lay eggs are very attractive prey, for example.

Insects are taken year-round whenever they are available. On their wintering grounds, orioles can often be found gleaning for insects on foliage and poking into flowers. In Mexico, Black-headed Orioles are among the very few birds that visit the overwintering roosts of Monarch butterflies to feed on these migratory insects. They have even developed a strategy to deal with the Monarch's toxic composition. The birds avoid poisoning by not eating the Monarch's cuticle, the outer covering of the abdomen where it stores most of the noxious chemicals. Rather, they slit open the butterflies and eat only the internal tissues.

FEASTING ON FRUIT

The best way to get lots of food—and to get it quickly—is to eat whatever is abundant. This is exactly what North American orioles do when fruit becomes available on their breeding grounds (and later on their wintering grounds). In summer, smaller fruits, such as raspberries, elderberries, huckleberries, juneberries, chokecherries, and mulberries are commonly eaten, depending on the locality. Baltimore Orioles in Kansas, for example, often get their tail feathers stained purple from the juice of the mulberries they ate, and then excreted, in abundance. Small fruits are often fed to nestlings and fledglings. Baltimore Orioles are sometimes regarded as a nuisance around grapevines or when they peck into ripe tomatoes or strip the pods off pea plants (they more than make up for these "faults" by the number of pest insects they consume, however).

Apricots, grapes, and figs are also eaten on the breeding grounds or as the birds pass through an area during migration. In desert habitats, Scott's Orioles eat the fruits of cactus, agave, and yucca. Not only do these provide energy, they are also an important source of water. On the wintering grounds, Orchard Orioles seem particularly fond of the fruit of the mistletoe.

All species will eat oranges and other citrus fruits wherever they can find them, especially at feeders. These larger fruits are often eaten by using a particular style of feeding knowing as gaping. Members of the family Icteridae, which includes the orioles, are known for their particularly strong jaw musculature—the muscles that control the operation of the bill are modified in such a way to allow the birds to open their beaks with unusual strength. They use this adaptation for a variety of purposes. It allows them to insert their bill into soil, bark, a flower, a stem—or a fruit—and then forcibly open it, creating a hole. This allows them to suck the juice out of an orange or the pulp out of an apricot, or example, or to reach insects inaccessible to other songbirds. Bullock's Orioles have even been observed using gaping to reach the internal tissues of tent caterpillars, which can then be withdrawn without the need to consume the hairy outer skin.

It is appropriate that many of the fruits orioles search for become particularly abundant later in the summer, when the birds are preparing for a long migratory journey south. While high-protein foods are vital for growing youngsters and promoting feather development, the high sugar content in ripe fruit is more efficiently converted into fat, large reserves of which must be accumulated before migration. Some neotropical migrants almost double their weight before they begin their migratory trips and are sometimes down to skin and bones by the time they reach their winter destination. In fact, some must burn muscle tissue to ensure that they cover the last few miles.

THE IMPORTANCE OF NECTAR

Most of us know that hummingbirds have a fondness for nectar, but many people are surprised to learn that all of the North American orioles (as well as many of the tropical members of the genus) also regularly consume nectar. They do so whenever and wherever they can find it—either in flowers or from feeders. Bullock's Orioles in California, for example, seem particularly fond of the nectar of the blue gum eucalyptus tree, from which they take pollen as well. Bullock's and other orioles also take nectar from agave plants, among other species. Baltimore and Orchard Orioles have often been observed feeding on nectar from flowering trumpet creepers, and they seem to prefer mature flowers, which have the highest nectar content.

It should be noted that the orioles are not doing the flowers any favors by taking their nectar. Flowers offer nectar as an enticement for insects, especially bees, to visit them. When the insects do, they pick up pollen grains from the male parts of the plants. Seeking more nectar, these insects then visit other plants, typically of the same species, where they often brush against the female parts of the plant, dropping off the pollen they picked up and allowing the plant to reproduce. In most cases, orioles do not act as pollinators when they visit flowers. They are thus often referred to as "nectar robbers" since they take their reward without performing any service. Usually, they pierce the nectar-containing parts of the plant and use gaping to create an opening through which they can lap up the nectar. Since this method of feeding bypasses the plant's reproductive parts, the orioles do not pick up or drop off any pollen and thus don't assist in the pollination process.

Fortunately, orioles are not *always* the bad guys. Orchard Orioles, for example, seem to be the most effective pollinators of a large and common tree known as *Erythrina fusca.* On their wintering grounds, Orchard Orioles visit this plant quite frequently, and they open the flower in such a way that they do pick up pollen as they get the nectar. Interestingly, this plant blooms just at the time of year when Orchard Orioles are most abundant in the area. Also fascinating is the fact that only adult male orioles, which are burnt orange in color, open the flowers; they aggressively exclude females and young males, both of which have greenish-olive plumage. Odder still is that the burnt orange of these males is exactly matched by a portion of the *Erythrina* flower that is only visible when the flower has been opened correctly and drained of nectar. Eugene Morton of the Smithsonian Institution has proposed that the color of the flower is a signal that both attracts and repels male Orchard Orioles. Its presence entices them to enter but then signals them that the nectar has been taken and thus encourages them to move on to another flower in another plant of the same species.

Although they take it year-round, nectar forms a particularly important part of the oriole's diet in winter. Analysis of the nectar from various types of plants has shown that it can contain substantial levels of various amino acids, the building blocks of proteins. It thus provides many of the same nutrients as insect food does and is usually considerably higher in sugars, which supply quick energy.

Particularly nectar-rich food sources are sometimes defended by individual orioles or even small flocks. There are reports, for example, of Baltimore Orioles aggressively challenging hummingbirds when they feed on certain types of flowers. Bullock's Orioles have been observed defending *Erythrina breviflora* flowers against wrens and tanagers. In Mexico, Bullock's Orioles have also been observed being displaced by both Black-vented and Streak-backed Orioles while feeding at *Pseudobombax ellipticum,* the shaving brush tree.

OTHER FOODS

Although insects, fruit, and nectar make up the major portion of the diet of most orioles, there are a few food items that don't fit into these categories. Spiders, for example, are commonly eaten, as are terrestrial snails and slugs if they present themselves. In hotter climes, small lizards can be

Flowers provide most of the nectar orioles need, but they will readily eat artificial nectar—sugar water—offered in backyard hummingbird feeders or specially made oriole feeders.

a rare tasty treat. Baltimore Orioles have been observed apparently enjoying leaves and feeding them to their offspring along with more traditional insect fare. When poking in flowers for insects or nectar, orioles may also take seeds, particularly when they are newly formed. In early May, the buds of various plants are occasionally eaten as well.

In one study of the Bullock's Oriole's eating habits, it was discovered that many individuals had eggshells in their guts. In fact, similar studies on a variety of species have shown that most, if not all, birds eat eggshells. Although some species are egg predators and eat what is inside the egg, as well as the shell itself, most songbirds, including orioles, eat only the shells. Most commonly this involves consuming at least some of the shells of their own eggs after they hatch. Calcium is a vital part of the diet for birds; it is needed for bone formation and the normal functioning of nerves and muscles. Female orioles may need to replenish their calcium reserves after egg laying to compensate for what they may have reallocated into egg production from other body parts. Calcium is also particularly important during the few weeks of growth. Before they hatch, developing birds obtain some calcium from the eggs that surround them, but after they hatch, their only supply is what their parents feed them. The food that young songbirds receive during their first few days in the nest is first eaten by their parents and then regurgitated into begging mouths. This provides the perfect opportunity for parents to eat, mix, and then give back a bit of the calcium from their babies' own eggs.

One of the oddest reports on oriole foods relates to observations of a Bullock's Oriole on South Farallon Island, California, eating a hummingbird. Whether the oriole had actually killed the hummingbird was unknown. Observers note that the prey could have been found dead. They also noted that there is not much food available for land birds on South Farallon. Few of the things an oriole typically eats are available, particularly in August, when the hummingbird was consumed.

FEEDING ORIOLES

Unlike most birds that come to feeders, orioles will not be particularly satisfied with the standard fare of seeds. There are plenty of other options, however, that will attract orioles to your yard and help them raise their young, cope with the stress imposed by a long migration, and survive the winter.

Nectar is a big hit with orioles during all seasons. Sugar water can easily be used as a substitute for the real thing. It won't provide the proteins found in some types of nectar but it will supply much-needed energy. Somewhere between one-sixth to one-third of a cup of sugar to one cup of water is within the range of most natural nectars. It is a good idea to make the mixture on the strong side during cool months, when birds need more energy. Make it weaker in the summer when fluid is useful to prevent dehydration. You don't need to add food coloring to the mixture. In fact, this probably isn't desirable since the chemicals used to produce the color are not beneficial and might even be harmful.

Honey is not a good substitute for sugar. Bacteria and fungi are more likely to grow in a honey-water mixture than in a sugar-water one. Even with sugar, though, homemade nectar can soon be home to various kinds of detrimental bacteria, especially in warm weather. The mixture must be changed frequently: every two days is a good target to aim for in summer, a little longer during cooler seasons. Some experts recommend boiling the water before mixing in sugar to reduce the chance that it contains dangerous microorganisms. Hot water will also dissolve the sugar more easily. Just be sure that it has cooled sufficiently before setting it out for the birds.

It's a good idea to make new nectar each time you fill up a feeder. One way to decrease waste is to use two or three smaller feeders instead of one large one, which may not get emptied soon enough. Spreading the feeders out in various locations will also help reduce territorial interactions among the users, thereby ensuring that more birds get to feed.

Standard hummingbird feeders are designed for small hovering birds that may land only briefly while feeding and so need only tiny perches. They are not really suitable for orioles, which are much larger and heavier than hummers. Many types of commercial oriole bird feeders are now available, however. Most are orange, on the theory that the birds seem particularly attracted to that color; they are generally flatter than hummingbird feeders and have more substantial perches. Many are also designed to hold cut pieces of oranges or other fruit, another favorite oriole food. Remember that feeders should be washed regularly with hot, soapy water to prevent the growth of bacteria. A bleaching, or soaking in boiling water, every so often is also a good idea, although you need to rinse the feeder carefully if bleach is used.

Ants and wasps will be attracted to filled oriole feeders. Ants can be held at bay with a water-filled device that keeps them from reaching the nectar. Special wasp traps can be used to control numbers of the various kinds of hornets and wasps that plague feeders. It is wise to put these traps out early before the population of stinging visitors gets too large.

As noted, orioles also love fruit. Grapes, currants, apples, bananas, and oranges are all excellent choices for oriole food. Platform feeders provide a stable and large enough surface for this fare. Like nectar, fruit can spoil quickly, particularly in warm weather; it should not be left out for more than a couple days. In the southern states, orioles may be more accustomed to coming to feeders for their fruit than they are in the more temperate parts of their range. It only takes one or two individuals to discover the feeder before many more join in, however. Some people say that filling a tree with orange halves (stuck securely on twigs) or arranging a number of orange halves on fence posts (stuck to pegs made of long nails) creates a conspicuous feeding area that attracts birds that might miss a single small feeder.

Grape jelly is another oriole favorite. It combines the energy of sugar with the color and taste of grapes. Some orioles will also come for orange marmalade or various types of jam, but jelly seems to be the most attractive. Some observers report that birds will continue to visit feeders for this type of food long after they have stopped being interested in oranges. The jelly should be offered a spoonful or so at a time in small containers such as the lids of jars. The containers shouldn't be very deep; the jelly gets very sticky, especially after it has been out for a while, and could really make a mess of feathers. As the sugars in jelly are more concentrated than they are in nectar or fruit, it's a good idea to be sure birds have a source of clean drinking water nearby.

Nectar and fruit and jelly are especially useful to offer in the spring or late fall, when birds need energy to sustain or continue their migratory journey. In fact, depending on where you live, this may be the only time you attract orioles to your yard. Many people who do not live in an area in which orioles commonly nest still enjoy their visits during migration. In the summer, when they are feeding nestlings or fledglings, however, orioles really need the protein provided by insect food. Mealworms are a good source of these nutrients and are available in pet stores or ordered in bulk online. The worms can easily be offered at feeders as long as they are in a dish deep enough to keep them from crawling away.

Suet is another good option as oriole fare. Although we may usually think of offering it only to birds like chickadees, nuthatches, and wood-

Halved fruits such as oranges attract orioles throughout the breeding season.
If you offer such treats, it's important to throw out or replace uneaten fruit
before it becomes smelly or moldy.

peckers that overwinter in cold climes, suet is actually eaten with enthusi-
asm by a variety of birds—including orioles—year-round. You can buy
ready-made suet cakes for birds in grocery stores or bird centers or get fat
trimmings from a butcher. Suet can be stuffed into suet cages or mesh bags
in its raw state or melted down, strained, poured into some sort of mold,
and chilled. Rendered suet stays solid and keeps much better than the raw
material; only rendered suet should be offered during warm weather.

Calcium supplements are a great idea for oriole feeders. This nutrient
is always in high demand, especially for females, who need an abundance

of it to produce the shells of their eggs. In addition, in some parts of North America, acid rain has leached calcium from the soil, making it less available in the grit birds ingest to help them digest their food and in the exoskeletons of the invertebrates they eat. The result seems to be that some species of birds are laying more fragile eggs with thinner shells. Providing calcium-rich eggshells at feeders can help compensate.

Since eggs can harbor the bacteria that cause salmonella, shells that are fed to birds should either come from hard-boiled eggs or be baked at 250 degrees F (120 degrees C) for at least twenty minutes. Once sterilized and cooled, the shells should be crushed into pieces less than a quarter inch in diameter. Crushed oyster shells purchased at pet stores can also be put out at feeders as a source of calcium and or grit.

3

An Oriole Year

Baltimore Oriole
Took one look at that mercury, forty below
No life for a lady
To be draggin' her feathers around in the snow
Leaving me blue, off she flew . . .

—GEORGE HARRISON

Orioles, like other migratory species, spend most of their time doing one of three things: nesting in temperate regions, wintering in neotropical environments, or flying between the two. An examination of an oriole's year in detail illustrates how it survives and thrives in the wild. We'll look first at the Baltimore Oriole and then the Bullock's Oriole to see how it's similar and how it differs. Brief summaries of the Orchard Oriole's, Scott's Oriole's, and Hooded Oriole's years follow.

BALTIMORE ORIOLE

SPRING

The Baltimore Oriole is considered a medium- to long-distance migrant. It leaves its wintering grounds in Central America and northern South America very early. The first migrants depart Panama, for example, the first week in February, although a few birds may still remain into May. From March through May, Mexico is filled with streams of transient orioles. The first of these migrants arrive in Texas and southern Missouri in mid-April and in Ohio and New Jersey in late April, although some are still arriving in late

The male Baltimore Oriole has unmistakable black and orange plumage in spring, with a black head, neck, upper breast, rump, and outer tail feathers. The black wings sport a single white bar. The rest of the feathers are bright orange. It's a medium-sized oriole, generally 7 to 8 inches long.

The female Baltimore Oriole is much duller than the male, even in the spring. It's a drab olive above with yellowish feathers below and on the rump. Dusky black can be seen on the head, neck, back, and wings, which sport two white bars.

Immature Baltimore Orioles are similar in appearance, and size, to the female.

May. The farther north birds must travel, the longer it takes them to get there. Orioles usually make their first appearance in Massachusetts and southwest Nova Scotia in early May and central Ontario and Alberta in mid- to late May.

The migratory journey in spring occurs mainly along the Atlantic slope of Mexico and Central America. Many Baltimore Orioles cross the Gulf of Mexico during spring and are found infrequently on islands in the West Indies and north of South America. Occasionally, they must hop a ride (perhaps inadvertently) on a boat (the first records of this species in Newfoundland are of two birds that mistakenly traveled to that northerly shore on a boat). Relatively few Baltimore Orioles move up the west coast of North America in spring. They are described as being regular but rare in California from mid-May to early June, and there are about twenty-five records in total from coastal Oregon, most of which are spring migrants.

At least some migration occurs at night. Reports of Baltimore Orioles killed at lighted towers attest to this, as does the fact that new migrants often appear first thing in the morning. In fact, many migrants seem to depart at or just after nightfall and fly until after dawn. For much of the journey, they tend to travel in small flocks in which ages and sexes are mixed, although males have a tendency to migrate before most females.

The Baltimore Oriole is widespread throughout much of eastern and central North America.

The **Baltimore Oriole,** the state bird of Maryland, was initially named the "Baltimore-bird" by Mark Catesby, an English naturalist who wrote and illustrated the first published account of the flora and fauna of North America. He gave the bird this name because its colors were the same as those of Cecil Calvert, the second Lord Baltimore and the Englishman who created the colony of Maryland. The "oriole" part of the name did not come along until 1785, when the Latin name used by taxonomists was translated. Because it resembled the orioles of Europe, the Baltimore-bird was placed in the same genus, which came to be known as *Oriolus.* By the time ornithologists figured out that the North American orioles were not related to the European birds, the name had stuck. (The Major League Baseball team was named for the bird, by the way, not the other way around.)

Older males (at least two years of age and in full breeding plumage) arrive first on the breeding grounds, preceding one-year-old males by a few days and females by about a week.

Although they have been practicing their songs periodically during migration and even on the wintering grounds, males really launch into full voice when they arrive in the area where they will attempt to nest. Once there they use their songs to stake out and defend a territory into which they will try to attract a mate. Although it now seems to us that they are home, they will actually spend only about a third of their year on their breeding grounds.

SUMMER

As they move northward, orioles look out for suitable breeding habitat. Ideally, this involves a woodland edge in a riparian area—along streams, lakes, and creeks. This type of habitat provides the ideal place to nest as well as find flowers (which harbor insects and nectar), abundant insects, and, later, fruit. Like most orioles, the Baltimore Oriole is a fairly adaptable species; many nest in urban and suburban parks, in residential areas with large trees, and along roadsides or trees bordering agricultural fields. In Ontario, 318 nest records included 96 in what were described as wooded areas (mostly deciduous, rarely mixed); 63 in gardens; 55 along the shores of rivers, lakes, or wetlands; 47 on roadsides; 30 in fields containing scattered trees or hedgerows; 13 in parks, school yards, or playing fields; 11 in orchards; and 3 in heath-tamarack bogs.

The Baltimore Oriole once had a preference for elm trees as nesting sites, at least in eastern North America. With the loss of so many elms in the late 1960s and '70s, their tastes have shifted. In the Great Plains and prairies, they favor cottonwood trees along streams. Farther north, aspen, poplar, or birch trees are most often chosen, especially those in open woodlands or parks and hedgerows. The breeding range of the Baltimore Oriole is large, spanning much of the United States and southern Canada east of the Rocky Mountains. The bird nests as far north as the extreme northeast portion of British Columbia and northern Alberta, down to southern Mississippi, central Louisiana, and northeast Texas.

Many orioles, of course, already have a destination in mind when they leave their wintering grounds. Banding studies have shown that many birds return to where they nested in a previous year. In western Massachusetts, one of three females banded in 1966 returned in 1967 and nested 160 yards from where she had built her nest the previous year. In south-central Kansas, nine of twenty-eight males that were two or more years old returned to breed in the study area the next year, as did seventeen of thirty-five first-year males and thirteen of thirty-three of females. The average distance between the nests these individuals built in the two years was 107 yards. Given that only about 50 percent of neotropical migrants survive from one year to the next, these data imply that if birds can return to their old stomping grounds, they do. Fledglings, on the other hand, seem to disperse—there are few if any records of orioles returning to breed where they hatched.

Once the nest site has been established, Baltimore Orioles seem to defend what are referred to as B-type territories—mainly the space around its nest or nest tree. They feed anywhere from 50 to 100 yards away from the nest, in areas where their neighbors are also foraging. Thus, although nesting territories don't overlap, what might be termed the birds' "activity spaces" often do, especially in ideal habitat where nesting density is reasonably high. Although the territory is originally established by the male, its mate also plays a role in its defense, especially against intrusions by other females.

Baltimore Orioles are described as being "socially monogamous." This means males "officially" mate with only one female (ditto for females). Although a pair appears to be faithful to each other, some extrapair copulation may still occur. And the pair bond seems to last only one season. When both members of a banded pair of birds have returned to the same breeding grounds, they have always obtained new mates.

Although the sex ratio seems to be equal at birth, the total number of males in most carefully studied Baltimore Oriole populations exceeds the number of females. Thus, while all females and older males become paired, only some of the younger males obtain mates; the remainder make up a population of "floaters" that are available to replace any older males that die over the summer. During breeding season, these floater males learn about breeding grounds and the mating process and may attempt to obtain "illicit" matings as well.

Perhaps because of the potential for cuckoldry, male orioles engage in a variety of behaviors that seem to reinforce the pair bond. They make quite elaborate displays involving songs—bowing and hopping from branch to branch—in order to attract a mate and just before copulation. They also guard their mates quite closely, especially during their most fertile period, which is about the time of egg laying. In fact, throughout the nest-building and egg-laying periods, the male orioles spend a great deal of time foraging or perched near their nests or mates. They also occasionally feed incubating or brooding females. During three experiments in which a researcher mimicked intrusion by playing another male's song, the territory owners mounted and quickly copulated with their mates, without either mate making the elaborate displays traditionally seen before this activity. In each of these instances the male might have been attempting to reduce the effects of possible cuckoldry by trying to ensure that it was his sperm that fertilized his mate's ova.

Until the eggs hatch, female orioles take the dominant role in nesting. After courting and choosing a mate, the female selects the nest site within or at the edge of the male's territory. She alone builds the nest, starting construction one to two weeks—or even a few days—after arrival on the breeding grounds. In Arkansas and Kentucky, nest building begins before May in some years, whereas in Pennsylvania this activity is at its peak in late May. In most states, nest building is under way by mid-month. It occurs slightly later in more northern parts of the species' range.

A Baltimore Oriole nest is a wondrous thing. Woven by the female out of plant fibers, as well as yarn, string, and other found materials, and lined with soft down, the baglike structure often holds together over the winter, although it's rarely used again the following spring.

The Baltimore Oriole's nest is usually built near the tip of one of the outer branches of a large, spreading tree. Sometimes it is nearer the trunk, especially in the Great Plains, which may be related to higher winds in this area. Studies have shown that in the east, where predation pressure from squirrels is higher, nests are attached to thinner, less squirrel-accessible branches on average; they tend to hang from thicker, more wind-resistant branches in the west.

The nests are usually high off the ground and hidden by leaves. In Ontario, records of four hundred nests showed that they ranged in height from about 1 to 30 yards, the largest number being from about 5 to 10 yards off the ground.

Nest construction can take up to fifteen days but is usually completed within a week, sometimes in only four or five days. According to one author, there are three stages to nest building. First, the outer bowl is constructed of flexible plant, animal, or human-made fibers (yarn, string, even cellophane tape and fishing line have been used). This provides support for the entire structure. Next, springy fibers that help maintain the shape of the nest are woven into the inner bowl. In both of these stages, the female usually only brings one fiber at a time, which she works into the nest. Finally, a soft lining, usually of plant material, is added. Often these materials are stolen from nearby nests, active or inactive.

In 1935, Francis Hobart Herrick provided a wonderfully detailed description of the oriole's nest-building process: "The first strands of bast, which are apt to be long, are wound around the chosen twig rather loosely with one or more turns. . . . [S]ubsequent modes of treatment tend to draw these threads tighter, and as their free ends are brought together, other fibers are added . . . [until] a loose pendant mass or snarl of fibrous material . . . is slowly formed. . . . Clinging to the principal twig, hanging often with head down, and holding the thread, the bird makes a number of rapid thrust-and-draw movements with her mandibles. . . . [T]here was certainly no deliberate tying of knots, yet, knots were in reality being made in plenty . . . The work was all fairly loose at first, yet naturally, some of the threads became drawn more tightly than others. . . . The irregularity of the weave of the finished work shows conclusively that the stitching is a purely random affair."

After two or three days, a tangled mass of fibers, from which many strands dangle freely, hangs from the twigs that will eventually support the finished nest. This typically becomes one side of the nest. Often working from what will later be the inside of the nest, the female weaves in additional twigs for support, outlines the frame of the remaining sides, and then continues to work in new material as well as incorporate the previously dangling threads to fill in the walls. In the last stages of construction, she appears to settle in the bottom of the nest, shakes, resettles, and repeats this process in what seems to be an attempt to shape the overall structure. Later, she will often poke at the nest from inside during incubation and brooding, perhaps reweaving or adding material.

The end result is a pensile bag 3 to 4 inches deep. It is larger at the bottom than the top; the nest cup portion is about 3 to 4 inches in diameter and the opening at the top about 2 to 3 inches in diameter. Although the nests are strong and tend to last well (many survive the winter), there are few reports of nests being reused. In general, a new nest is built for each nesting attempt. In some cases, old nests are reused by other species, such as House Wrens.

Although these nests look warm, studies have shown that they are no better insulated than those of other cup-nesting species. In colder parts of the oriole's breeding range, exposure still causes the death of significant numbers of young, either while they are still in the egg or when they are nestlings. As well, the hanging nature of the nests may make them more susceptible to falling when supporting twigs break in storms. During a study in western Massachusetts, about 30 percent of all eggs and nestling losses were attributed to storms that caused nests to fall. A similar proportion of losses were due to egg desertion or nestling starvation (desertion of nests is common when the weather is unusually cold or rainy).

Typically, the female starts laying at the same time she is putting the finishing touches on the nest lining. She lays one egg per day, beginning to incubate when the last or second last one is laid. Baltimore Oriole eggs have a pale grayish-white background on which brown, lavender, or black lines form irregular streaks or blotches. The blotching tends to be denser at the large end of the egg. Three to seven eggs are laid, with four or five being the most common clutch size.

Most females start to lose the feathers on their belly one to two weeks after they arrive on the breeding grounds. By the time incubation begins, they have a bare incubation patch that can effectively keep the eggs warm. The female incubates for twelve days on average (depending on the number of eggs laid), usually for fifteen and forty-five minutes at a time, interspersed with breaks of up to twenty minutes, during which she forages. She roosts on the nest at night.

The male typically inspects the nest contents during egg laying and spends a lot of his time feeding, preening, or sitting near the nest during incubation. Some males bring the odd food item to their incubating mates but otherwise aren't really much help until the young hatch, typically over a two- to three-day period. Then the male springs into action. Although only the females brood the new nestlings, the males start bringing food for the young. In fact, even though some of the offspring in the nest may not be his, the male takes a more-or-less equal role in caring for the nestlings, making about 45 percent of the feeding trips and carrying away fecal sacs as often as the females do. During a study of thirty-four nests conducted in Kansas, the male and female together made an average of thirteen trips each hour, bringing food for the young. If her mate dies, a female can increase her feeding rate dramatically to compensate for his absence. She can thus raise her young alone, although the energy cost may compromise her chances of surviving migration.

For the first few days, the parents feed their young by regurgitating food they have already eaten. Later, they will place food in the open mouths of their young. Sometimes a parent will remove, rearrange, and replace a large item placed into a nestling's gaping mouth several times before the nestling finally takes it. Caterpillars and the soft parts of other insects are commonly given to the young, as are fruits when they become abundant. The parents work at keeping the nest clean. Feces produced by the nestlings are enclosed in sacs that the parents carry away and drop at a distance from the nest (typically they eat these sacs for the first few days after the young hatch). During the last couple days they spend at home, the young sometimes stand and defecate over the rim of the nest.

When they hatch, young orioles are nearly naked, their pink skin sparsely covered with whitish down. Their eyes are closed and they weigh approximately only 0.07 ounce. The youngest nestling, which hatches a day or two after the others, often dies or is much smaller than its siblings when they fledge. By the time they are ready to leave the nest about twelve or thirteen days after hatching, the young have grown to essentially adult size. Young that leave before reaching ten days of age typically do not survive. The grown birds weigh around 1 ounce and have legs that are as long as those of their parents. Their wing and tail feathers are stubby, allowing

Male and female orioles generally divide the chore of feeding their nestlings evenly. Oriole chicks grow quickly and are ready to leave the nest twelve or thirteen days after hatching, although they are still fed by their parents for another couple weeks.

for only short flights, at least for the first few days after fledging. The young are probably most vulnerable to predators at this time. Since their beaks are short and somewhat soft, the young orioles still need to be fed for a while after leaving the nest.

When not begging from their parents, the young become quiet and inconspicuous, and it is often very difficult to observe their movements. It appears, however, that they don't become fully independent for another couple of weeks. The parents continue to care for them, dividing the labor for the first few days. In all parts of their range, Baltimore Orioles are known to be single-brooded, meaning that they only raise one batch of young per season. If a nest is preyed upon or otherwise lost early in the nesting cycle, the female may build a new nest and produce a replacement clutch. Very late renesting attempts are commonly deserted in the egg stage, however; the time to produce young that will be able to survive the long migration is too short, and nesting late in the season would be a waste of energy. Surviving the trip south also requires that parents concentrate on acquiring fat reserves rather than working off calories caring for young.

About two weeks after leaving the nest (in mid- to late July, depending on the locality) the immature birds start leaving the area of their nest tree, traveling more widely. By August, small flocks of these juveniles begin to form and move conspicuously around the breeding grounds—in contrast to their parents, who are quite solitary and secretive at this time as they undergo prebasic molt. The juveniles probably begin their migration in late August, shortly after their parents have left.

FALL

Throughout their range, Baltimore Orioles begin fall migration in July and August, after the prebasic molt is complete or almost so. The peak of migration in central Ontario is July 26 to August 30 compared to August 20 to late September farther south, at Cape May, New Jersey. It occurs from late August to early September (with stragglers through late September) in Missouri and in late August to early October in Texas.

In the fall, most birds migrate overland through Mexico. They principally travel along the Atlantic slope, as they do in spring, but some are also seen in northern Yucatan. A relatively small number take the overwater route to the Caribbean Islands. Even fewer seem to travel through the western United States in fall than in spring. There are very few records from coastal Oregon in fall, and the species is described as a very rare transient in California from August through September. Baltimore Orioles begin to arrive on the wintering grounds by late August—in fresh plumage. The average fall arrival date in San Jose, Costa Rica, is September 24. Migrants typically reach Panama by the end of September and Colombia in mid-October.

More oriole flocks are observed during fall migration than in spring. This may be due to the presence of juveniles, which tend to flock more than the adults. At this time of the year, they are not easy to distinguish from females, and the age and sex makeup of these flocks is thus uncertain.

WINTER

Winter finds most Baltimore Orioles in the southern half of Mexico, south through Central America to northern Venezuela to north and west Colombia. Some choose the West Indies for their winter destination, where they can be found from Cuba and Jamaica east to the Virgin Islands. A few end up scattered in northwest Ecuador, Puerto Rico, and Bermuda. Banding records show that many birds winter repeatedly in the same location. Of course, wintering in the same location depends on the habitat they found there the previous year being the same or not altered so much that the birds must search elsewhere for sustenance.

Every year, some birds stay behind in the United States, and this number is probably increasing as the global climate warms. Baltimore Orioles winter regularly in Florida and extreme southern Georgia. They can also be found, in numbers that decline the farther north one goes, along the Atlantic coast to New England. There are records of birds surviving the winter as far north as Nova Scotia (but not without their being brought inside for the coldest weeks of the year, which isn't really the same thing as making it on their own). For all these northern birds, the use of feeders is required for survival. Orioles also winter regularly in the coastal lowlands of California. Odd birds are thus found farther north along the western side of the continent, into Oregon. And a few perhaps unhealthy birds linger in the interior of eastern North America as far north as southern Ontario.

Orioles that make it to their wintering grounds look for habitat that provides the food and shelter they need. In much of their winter habitat, they seek shade coffee or cacao plantations where the overstory trees provide hiding places, flowers, fruit, and insects. Their favored trees include various species in the genera *Inga* and *Erythrina* as well as *Gliricidia sepium*, all of which are commonly found on Latin American farms and as street and park trees. The Baltimore Oriole is as adaptable in winter as it is in summer; it can be found in native woodlands—typically less dense coniferous or deciduous woods, depending on the area—as well as in scrub habitats and gardens.

Their main criteria for good habitat is, of course, the presence of food. Orioles prefer flowering trees, which provide all three of their required dietary elements: insects, fruit, and nectar. There are some reports of the species aggressively defending particularly rich nectar sources from other birds, such as hummingbirds, but such behavior seems to be rare. In general, wintering orioles are neither aggressive nor particularly gregarious during the day. They tend to feed alone or in small groups of two to five individuals.

In winter, orioles have been observed probing termite runs on the underside of tree branches and eating oranges by pecking small holes in the peel and then gaping, eventually hollowing out the inside, or by eating fruits already opened by woodpeckers. They also rather inexpertly eat the fruit of the common gumbo-limbo tree by grabbing the nutlets with their mouths, removing the skin, and manipulating it to extract the pulp.

At night, the oriole does seek out comrades. It roosts communally, with groups of twenty or more Baltimore Orioles of both sexes joining with a variety of other birds (often Orchard Orioles, kingbirds, or finches) to sleep well concealed in the foliage. In these sites they perch on branches sometimes less than 3 yards from the ground and sleep with their heads turned back and buried in fluffed plumage.

Males do sing in winter, although their songs are described as being much shorter, simpler, and less frequent than those heard on the breeding grounds. In Panama and other parts of the wintering range, observers say that no singing is heard until March or April as the time approaches to head back to the breeding grounds. During winter, singing and being attractive to members of the opposite sex are much less important than eating: the journey north requires large fat reserves that will sustain the birds during the long springtime flight.

BULLOCK'S ORIOLE

SPRING

The Bullock's Oriole begins its northward journey from Mexico and Central America in March. It begins to arrive in southern Arizona in mid-March to early April, although in some years it appears during the first week in March. In California, the first migrants arrive March 10 through 15, although most pass through later in the month and into early April in the south and up to two weeks later in northern parts of the state. In fact, migratory individuals are still traveling through California until mid-May. In Oregon, the species arrives mid- to late April in the western valleys but later in the interior part of the state. They arrive in Colorado and through

The male Bullock's Oriole has roughly the same coloration as the Baltimore Oriole but the patterning is different. It has orange cheeks contrasting with its black crown and more of a white splotch on its dark wings. Its back and outer tail feathers are black. It, too, is a medium-sized bird, about 7 to 8 inches long.

The female Bullock's Oriole has drab olive plumage with yellow on the tail and light, buff-colored—not yellowish—feathers below. It sports two white bars on its dark wings.

Immature Bullock's Orioles are similar to the female, although young males sport black throats.

most of the Great Plains in early May. Bullock's Orioles appear in Canada in mid- to late May.

This species, like the Baltimore Oriole, is classified as a complete migrant, meaning that its wintering and breeding areas are completely separate. That said, there are birds present throughout the year along the coast in southern California. Although the birds seen in this area could be continuously replaced—any that winter there may move north in spring, their place taken by individuals that wintered farther south—some birds may actually be resident.

The migratory routes of this species cover western North America, mostly west of Louisiana. Unlike Baltimore Orioles, they do not cross the Gulf of Mexico. They seem to migrate mostly at night, often in small flocks.

SUMMER

For Bullock's Orioles, suitable breeding habitat is where there are trees large enough for nest sites as well as open areas in which to feed. Riparian woodlands are favored, with oak, cottonwood, sycamore, willow, and madrone

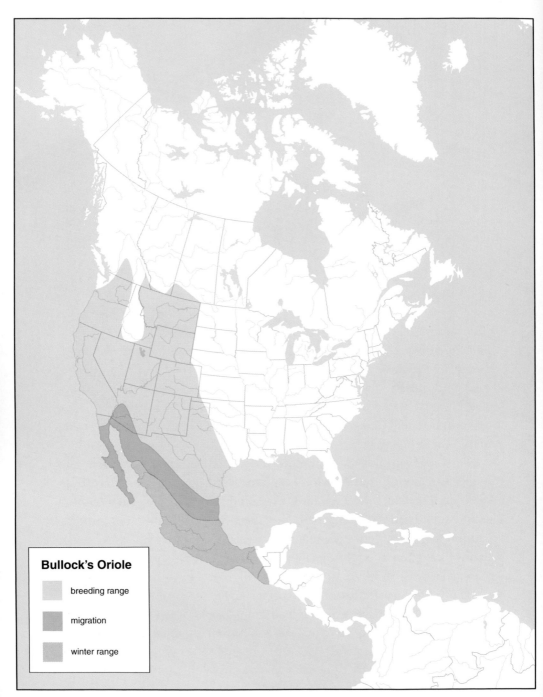

Bullock's Oriole

breeding range

migration

winter range

The Bullock's Oriole is the common species in much of western North America.

The **Bullock's Oriole** was named by William Swainson, an English naturalist who wrote several books in the first half of the 1800s, including one called *Fauna Boreali-Americana*, which established his reputation in North America. In it, he described and illustrated the Bullock's Oriole based on specimens that had been collected by another English traveler and natural historian, William Bullock. Two subspecies of the Bullock's Oriole have been described—the main, or "nominate," form, *Icterus bullockii bullockii*, which is a widespread breeding bird of the United States and Canada, and the smaller *Icterus bullockii parvus*, which breeds in the southwestern United States and western Mexico. The two do not differ substantially in appearance or behavior.

being the trees of choice. The species seems to prefer larger trees than are chosen by the Orchard Oriole, which has an overlapping breeding range.

Male Bullock's Orioles at least two years of age arrive on the breeding grounds first. Females start to arrive a few days later, and pairing occurs almost immediately. Orioles that have bred in a particular area show a high fidelity to that locale.

In much of its range, the Bullock's Oriole seems to be a solitary nester. It was long thought to defend A-type territories—meaning all its nesting and feeding areas. Recent studies have shown that while it may defend large territories in some locations, in general, it fights to hold only smaller B-type territories, the same as the Baltimore Oriole. Nests are often built near water, and several active nests may be built in close proximity. In California, for example, the maximum nesting density observed during one study was seventeen pairs in one 3.2 acre plot.

The Bullock's Oriole is typically monogamous—socially, at least. "Official" pairs stay together for one season only; in three cases in which both members of a banded pair have returned to the same breeding grounds used the previous year, all mated with other individuals. As with Baltimore Orioles, the sex ratio seems male-biased; whereas all females in studied populations nest, not all males are able to obtain mates. The younger males most often get left out.

The Bullock's Oriole's nest is pensile, typically suspended from a few thin branches. The nests can be very deep—a nest 15 inches long has been recorded in California. Usually, however, they are only a little deeper and wider than those of the Baltimore Oriole. The diameter of the opening is slightly smaller, though, which might provide more shade in the hotter environments typically frequented by Bullock's Orioles.

The female alone builds the nest (although there is one published description of a male helping out quite regularly with the building). They are usually placed 10 to 24 feet above the ground, although nests as low as 5 inches and as high as 50 feet have been reported. Like those of the Baltimore Oriole, they tend to be built on the leeward side of the nest tree, opposite the prevailing winds. The nest may take up to fifteen days to build.

The eggs, laid soon after the nest is complete, are pale bluish- or grayish-white, scrolled and speckled with fine purple or brown lines. They are laid at a rate of one per day. Clutches from three to seven eggs have been recorded, although the usual number of eggs is four or five.

As is true for other orioles, only the female Bullock's Oriole has a brood patch and incubates. The male frequently stays nearby, however, while she attends the eggs. Incubation takes eleven to twelve days, and the young hatch with the same scanty down as Baltimore Orioles. Except for the first few days, when the female broods, both parents feed the young and remove fecal sacs over the two-week nestling period.

Nest success for Bullock's Orioles tends to be higher than that for other cup-nesting birds but slightly lower than that for Baltimore Orioles. In northeast Colorado, for example, Bullock's females initiate their clutches later than Baltimore females, although both arrive on the same breeding grounds at a similar time. As a result, the Bullock's young fledge later and their nesting success is somewhat lower. Food availability may decline over the season, making later nests less successful.

Once they fledge, about two weeks after hatching, the young sometimes gather into small groups, which typically include individuals from several nests. In years when fledging is very synchronous—when many or most nests fledge at the same time—and foods such as grasshoppers are concentrated, these groups become what are called crèches; several families join their young and all are fed together by the parents. Fledged young in crèches have even been observed to be adopted by parents from a nearby nest. At this time, up to twenty birds are sometimes seen flying together to foraging sites, and up to a hundred individuals, including the young, have been seen at once in these locations. This phenomenon has been observed in both California and Washington. Formation of these crèches, which suggests cooperative breeding, needs further study.

FALL

Bullock's Orioles start to leave the breeding grounds in early July; most are gone from the arid habitats of Washington and California by the end of the month. In California as a whole, Bullock's Orioles pass through on their southward journey from late July to early September. Only a few stragglers are left in October. Most of them have left Colorado by the middle of September, and they are gone from British Columbia by the end of August. They are observed passing through the northern part of Mexico from July to September, and some are on their wintering grounds farther south by August.

The major difference between what Baltimore and Bullock's are doing at this time of year is related to when and where their major annual change of feathers—the prebasic molt—occurs. Almost all Baltimore Orioles complete this molt before they leave the breeding grounds. In contrast, Bullock's Orioles leave their nesting areas dressed in their old, worn feathers and molt somewhere along the route. Although this topic needs much more study, it appears that they probably stop their migratory journey in the southwest states to do this.

WINTER

The Bullock's Oriole spends the winter from central Mexico south to the highlands in central and western Guatemala. A few wintering orioles have been found in El Salvador and Costa Rica. The bird can also be found in small numbers along the coast of southern California and in the panhandle of Florida, a part of the state where Baltimore Orioles are *not* found in the winter. There are the usual occasional winter records for Oregon, Arizona, Texas, Alabama, and elsewhere, mostly in the west.

The male Orchard Oriole has a reddish, chestnut-colored appearance in spring, with a black head, neck, breast, back, and wings, which sport a single white bar. Orchard Orioles are smallish, generally 6 to 7 inches long. They are much less widespread than Baltimore Orioles but often more common in the south.

ORCHARD ORIOLE

Orchard Orioles leave their winter homes in March and April. Transient orioles can be seen in Texas from early April to early May. In Missouri, they usually arrive during the third week of April. Most arrive in Wisconsin from May 10 to 15. They arrive in West Virginia at the end of April and in Massachusetts in mid-May. Orchard Orioles were first discovered breeding in Manitoba in 1975. During the next three years, the first males showed up in this area on May 22, 28, and 16, respectively. In general, Orchard Orioles tend to arrive later in spring than other members of the genus *Icterus*.

For their breeding grounds, Orchard Orioles seem drawn to areas with scattered trees, which often occur in suburban areas, parks, around houses, or on farmlands. In general, compared with Baltimore and Bullock's Orioles, Orchard Orioles seem to prefer shorter trees with smaller canopies. It

As might be expected, the **Orchard Oriole** got its common name from its preference for orchards. The origin of its scientific name, *Icterus spurius,* is perhaps less dignified—the specific epithet does indeed mean spurious in English and is related to the bird's former common name, Bastard Baltimore Oriole (which stemmed from an error in identification: the female Baltimore Oriole was originally thought to be the male Orchard Oriole). The smallest of the North American orioles, the Orchard Oriole has a widespread breeding distribution east of the Rockies. A paler, ochre-colored version of this species, often called the Fuertes' Oriole or Ochre Oriole (*I. s. fuertesi*), breeds along the east coast of Mexico from southern Tamaulipas to southern Veracruz and winters from Guerrero to Chiapas. It has a shorter migratory journey but is otherwise very similar to the "main" chestnut-colored subspecies *I. s. spurius* in size and behavior. Despite this, recent genetic analysis suggests that they are actually quite distinct.

is still unclear to what extent Orchard Orioles defend their territories; this may vary with nesting patterns and the availability of resources. In some places, Orchard Orioles nest in colonies. In fact, the Orchard Oriole seems to be a very sociable bird—it will nest not only in the same tree as Baltimore or Bullock's Orioles but has been observed nesting near kingbirds, American Robins, and Chipping Sparrows. In general, it shows little aggression toward other species on its breeding grounds.

Pairs form soon after the females arrive in the spring, and nest building starts soon after. Unlike Baltimore and Bullock's Orioles, Orchard Orioles do not seem to shelter their nests by building on the leeward side of a tree, perhaps because their nests are more securely attached—they typically hang from the branches of a forked twig rather than one or more thin twigs. On average, female Orchard Orioles complete their nests in six days.

Egg laying starts soon after the nest is complete. The eggs range from light blue to bluish- or grayish-white with irregular purplish-brown to black markings. Four to six eggs are laid in each nest. Orchard Orioles have traditionally been described as single-brooded; although pairs would renest after the failure of their first brood, there was no evidence of pairs raising two broods in one season. Recently, however, in careful study of Orchard Oriole breeding populations in Maryland, eight of twenty-four Orchard Oriole pairs attempted a second brood, and seven of sixteen pairs that were successful in raising a first brood also successfully raised a second.

Although only the female incubates, the male has been observed guarding and bringing his mate food over the twelve- to fourteen-day incubation period. After the young fledge, they spend about a week in dense cover in the vicinity of the nest with both parents, who divide the care of the fledglings between them. In contrast to Baltimore Orioles, male Orchard Orioles leave the family group first.

In late summer, Orchard Orioles—in all cases, males before females and young of the year—start leaving Vermont and Massachusetts early in July, and all have gone by the end of the month. They are rarely seen in New York after August; the peak of migration in Cape May, New Jersey, occurs during the first two weeks of August. The species is gone from South Carolina and Georgia by mid-September, and the latest date it is usually seen in Florida is the middle of October. Farther inland, it starts to leave Minnesota by late July and is gone by the end of the first week in September. Migration occurs mainly at night. Birds traveling south seem to stick more to western routes than they do in the spring. More transients, particularly young females, are observed along the west coast of California in the fall than the spring, and many fewer are observed in Florida at this time of year.

The very first Orchard Orioles arrive on their wintering grounds in Honduras at the end of July and in Panama in mid-August, but most hold out until later than that. They are in Venezuela from September through March and in Colombia from early August until early May. In these areas, they seem to stick to fairly low elevations and prefer open forests, scrub, and cultivated areas, avoiding dense forests.

Orchard Orioles arrive on the wintering grounds sporting their old feathers, which they replace in the prebasic molt over the next couple months. The species is very sociable on its wintering grounds, roosting at night in large flocks. During the day, they commonly forage in groups of up to thirty.

The male Scott's Oriole has black and lemon-yellow plumage in the spring—black head, throat, upper breast, back, and wings with one white bar. The rump is yellow, as are the outer feathers on the otherwise black tail. The Scott's Oriole is medium-sized, about 7 to 8 inches long.

SCOTT'S ORIOLE

Most Scott's Orioles travel northward in March and April, arriving on their United States' breeding grounds in these months. There seems to be wide individual variation in travel times; perhaps because they don't have as far to go, they are under less pressure to get there quickly. Although many Scott's Orioles move northward along the Pacific coast of Baja California, once they reach the states, they appear to move inland and migrate along the desert slopes of mountains, in the kind of habitat they generally seek for breeding. As a result, they are rare along the coast of California in the spring. They migrate in flocks of ten to twenty, feeding on various kinds of flowers, especially those of the Ocotillo, en route. The brightly colored male Scott's Orioles arrive about a week before most of the females and younger males and start singing loudly, defending their small territories in preparation for mating.

The **Scott's Oriole** was given the scientific name *Icterus parisorum* in 1838 by Lucien Bonaparte, a French naturalist who had visited North America in the 1820s. The name commemorates brothers named Paris who, while doing business in Mexico, had financed the collection and transport to France of a large number of natural history specimens, including some of this oriole. A second attempt was made to name the species by Darius Couch, an American Civil War general who participated in the Mexican War and later lead a zoological expedition to Mexico. He called it *Icterus scottii,* in honor of Civil War General Winfield Scott (because the species already had been officially named, however, he had to settle for remembering the general in the species' common name, which is probably more used anyway). The bird is sometimes known as the Mountain Oriole or Desert Oriole.

In the summer, the Scott's Oriole is usually found in relatively higher elevations, usually in arid habitats, particularly the slopes of mountains that face deserts. It tends to avoid real deserts, where cacti are dominant and its preferred nesting trees are rare. In general, they look for areas where yuccas, piñon-juniper, Joshua trees, or oaks are common. Yucca flowers attract large numbers of insects, which are a principle part of the Scott's Oriole's diet. They may also obtain nectar from these flowers and get nutrients and moisture from the soft flower parts and fruiting pods. Like other orioles, Scott's are faithful to where they have bred before.

Few of their favorite nesting trees are tall. As a result, Scott's Oriole nests tend to be built lower to the ground than those of other orioles. In one west Texas study site, the average height of nests was about 10 feet off the ground. Nests are typically woven around overhanging leaves at the top of the tree. Many are suspended from the small crown of a yucca or attached to several dead leaves that hang down along the trunk. They are usually shaded and concealed by the leaves on the crown. The nests are made of fibrous materials—the dead parts of yucca plants with loose, peeling fibers are favored sources. The nests of Scott's Orioles are thus easy to distinguish from those of the Hooded Oriole where their ranges overlap: Hooded Orioles usually use material from green, living leaves, which often curl and warp and change into different colors than the yellow fibers used by Scott's Orioles. The use of cloth, paper, feathers, leaves, horsehair, and strips of plant bark in the lining of Scott's Oriole nests has been reported. Although there are a few anecdotal reports of males helping to build the nest, it is probably solely the job of the female, as in other orioles. Interestingly, Scott's females start many nests that they later abandon, particularly early in the breeding season.

The completed nests usually remain empty for two to four days before the female lays her first egg. She then proceeds to lay up to five (usually three) pale blue eggs irregularly streaked with black or brownish-purple markings. One egg is laid per day. Most females in a Texas study began incubating after laying the second (which was usually the penultimate) egg. The time between the laying of the last egg and the hatching of the first young was 12.9 days, on average. During this period, female orioles spend about half their time on the nest; the male sits nearby, accompanies the female when she leaves the nest, and sometimes brings her food.

In most cases, all the young hatch on the same day. Young Scott's Orioles grow quickly, from a fraction of an ounce at hatching to full weight when they leave the nest. The young are quiet for the first few days but later beg loudly when the parents visit. As fledging nears, the young can be heard quite a distance from the nest. As with other orioles, both sexes defend the nest against potential predators, brood parasites, and nest pirates, calling in alarm and flying at an enemy, sometimes actually striking it.

Female Scott's Orioles stop caring for their young about two weeks after the first brood fledges and almost immediately after the second. Several times, male orioles were observed feeding up to three young while their mates incubated the next clutch. The young seem dependent on their parents for the first two to three weeks after hatching, but since both parents are often feeding the next brood after this time, they must be able to shift for themselves.

Scott's Orioles do not have as high a rate of success as Baltimore or Bullock's Orioles on a per-nest basis. Although the majority of pairs probably only raise one set of young successfully each year, over two years of study, twenty-two of thirty-five of pairs that successfully raised one brood attempted a second—and four pairs that successfully raised two broods tried for a third. The high frequency of renesting means that some birds are still laying eggs into June and July. This is remarkable given that the prebasic molt in this species occurs on the breeding grounds in July and August and is apparently mostly complete before migration.

The Scott's Oriole is socially monogamous; there are no reports of polygyny or extrapair mating (but it may be only a matter of time and careful study before there are). Banding records indicate that pairs last only for one year.

Scott's Orioles start leaving their breeding areas from mid-July to early August, arriving in their wintering areas in late September. Migration along the Pacific coast is more common in the fall than in the spring; Scott's are considered to be regular, although rare, transients through this part of California from late July to November. They are sometimes seen in flocks at this time of year, too, but smaller groups are even more common and are often found at elevations higher than those at which they nest.

Little is known about what Scott's Orioles do on their wintering grounds in Mexico. They seem to stick to the same type of arid habitat they enjoy in the summer and eat the standard oriole fair of insects, fruit (especially the fruit of various kinds of cacti), and nectar. They are often observed in mixed species flocks, and, unlike other orioles, have not been observed defending rich sources of nectar in the winter. They do regularly feed on nectar from feeders.

HOODED ORIOLE

The Hooded Oriole migrates through the Mexican state of Sonora in large numbers from March to May. It arrives in southern California in mid-March and about two weeks later in the northern part of the state. During spring migration, it seems to wander north of its regular breeding range—there are records of birds in northern Nevada, Oregon, and Washington. Both Hooded and Scott's Orioles seem to be expanding their ranges northward.

Once called the "Palm Leaf Oriole," the Hooded Oriole seems drawn to palms and related trees for nesting. It is commonly found in dry habitats but at lower elevations than those favored by the Scott's Oriole—open woodlands, riparian areas in deserts and semideserts, and, increasingly, urban and suburban areas and parks. One factor in the bird's range extension in California is perhaps the widespread planting of ornamental fan palms. In the Rio Grande Valley of Texas as well as eastern Mexico, the Hooded Oriole is frequently found in patches of Texas ebony and mesquite trees.

The male Hooded Oriole in spring has a distinctive black face contrasting with a yellowish-orange crown, sides, and belly. Its wings—with a wide white bar— and tail feathers are black. The Hooded Oriole is slightly smaller than the Bullock's or Baltimore Orioles, generally around 7 inches in length.

Sites selected for nest building seem to vary. In California, the bird typically suspends its nests from the leaves of various kinds of trees: palms, bananas, sycamores, eucalyptus. Nests attached to buildings or other structures are more common today than in the past, perhaps because the orioles are found so often around human habitations.

Built by the female alone, in three to six days, the Hooded Oriole's nest is like those of other orioles. Often it is suspended from the underside of a palm or banana leaf. In this case, the female uses her bill to poke holes in the leaf so she can push fibers through it—in essence sewing the nest to the leaf. Various types of fibers are used: grass, strands of Spanish moss, threads pulled from the edges of green yucca or palmetto leaves, and so on. A new nest is typically constructed for each nesting attempt of the season, of which there are commonly two, sometimes three.

The namesake facial marking of the **Hooded Oriole** is actually a black bib—its name presumably makes reference to its orange "hood," which is actually contiguous with the orange on the side of its head and its breast. The scientific name of the species, *Icterus cuculattus*, confirms the importance of the hood for its namer, William Swainson, since *cuculla* is Latin for "hood." Five subspecies of Hooded Oriole are recognized by various authors, varying chiefly in bill length and the color of the male's plumage. The subspecies overlap extensively in appearance and geographical distribution.

Hooded Orioles lay three to five eggs, which are whiter than those of other orioles, although they bear the typical irregular brownish streaks and blotches. Incubation lasts for twelve to fourteen days. The young are cared for by both parents during a nestling period of about two weeks. Nest success in this species seems lower than for most orioles, which most authors attribute largely to the effects of cowbird parasitism.

Once fledged, the young usually remain near the nest for several days, cared for by their parents. Young Hooded Orioles undergo their first prebasic molt on the breeding grounds. Most Hooded Orioles leave northern California by early September and are gone from the southern part of the state by the middle of the month. The species starts to leave the lower Colorado River Valley around the third week of August. Migrants are common in Sonora in August and September. Most migratory Hooded Orioles seem to spend the winter within or near the range of nonmigratory Hooded Orioles that remain in Mexico all year, from the southern tip of Sonora south to central Oaxaca and in the east from southern Tamaulipas to Belize.

The bird favors a variety of winter habitats, including arid pine-oak woodlands, thorn forests, and urban areas. Like other orioles, it frequently forages on nectar in winter; individuals or groups of orioles will defend particularly rich sources against wrens, tanagers, and other species of orioles. Adult Hooded Orioles are thought to undergo their prebasic molt on their wintering grounds.

RESIDENT ORIOLES

The Altamira Oriole, Audubon's Oriole, and Spot-breasted Oriole remain in the same range year-round. They also share other features that differentiate them from the migratory North American species. In all three, plumage maturation is delayed for at least one year in both sexes, rather than just the males. All three sing regularly year-round, at least to a greater extent than do the migratory orioles. Females of the resident species sing songs that are generally similar to those of the males. The male and female Audubon's Orioles' songs in particular seem indistinguishable. In some parts of their range, these species seem to stay on or near their breeding territories all year. Although they can be seen foraging in small flocks, which often include other types of orioles, some experts believe they maintain year-round territories, although even during the breeding season territorial disputes are rare and not particularly aggressive.

The Spot-breasted Oriole is not native to the United States. The birds were first discovered nesting near Miami, Florida, in 1949; these were probably escaped captive birds. From there, it spread north and south and by 1970 had been seen from the Everglades to Lake Wales, 150 miles north of Miami. It is now present from Brevard County to Dade County. It's a tropical species, found from Mexico south through Central America to northern Costa Rica, typically in dry habitats. In Florida, it sticks to urban and suburban areas, especially those with flowering trees and bushes, breeding from April to late August. The species' numbers decline when Florida winters are particularly cold.

The Altamira and Audubon's Orioles are both primarily Mexican birds with geographic ranges that extend into Texas. Although they thus share several features, they are quite different. The Altamira Oriole is the largest member of the genus that breeds north of the Mexican border. It is not a shy bird—it often forages in the open. In contrast, the Audubon's Oriole is smaller and builds the most open nest of any North American Oriole. Their nests are also smaller relative to body size than the nests of other *Icterus* species. The Audubon's Oriole has a well-earned reputation for being secretive. Although it can be found at forest edges, it more commonly forages and nests in dense vegetation, making both the birds and their nests hard to find. In Texas, both species are limited to the southern part of the state, specifically the lower Rio Grande Valley.

The male Altamira Oriole in spring has a bright orange crown, neck, cheeks, and belly and a black throat, lores—the area between the eyes and the bill—wings, and tail. The wings sport an orange bar. This is a large oriole, generally 8 to 10 inches long.

The male Audubon's Oriole in spring has a lemon or greenish-yellow back, sides, and belly and an all-black head, upper breast, wings, and tail. It's generally slightly larger than the Bullock's Oriole, 8 to 9 inches long.

Surprisingly, these two species have been known to mate with each other, even though genetic studies of the genus indicate that they are not each other's closest relatives. The first mixed pair, the female of which built three nests but laid no eggs, was observed in 1988. Ten and eleven years later, a male hybrid mated and nested with a female Altamira Oriole in Hidalgo County, Texas. Two hybrids were observed in this same area in 2002, three in 2003 and 2005, and at least two in 2006. These birds had a mixed appearance, displaying features of both species. The nests were built by female hybrids and were much shorter than typical Altamira Oriole nests but more pensile than the usual Audubon's Oriole nest.

Six subspecies of Altamira Orioles have been described, based on differences in plumage color, body size, and geographical distribution. Four subspecies of the Audubon's Oriole are officially delineated, based more or less on the same features, although they tend to intergrade with each other.

4

Enemies and Friends

Songbirds generally live short lives. Probably only half of those that hatch survive to sexual maturity, and of those that breed in any one year, roughly half will still be alive to breed the following year. Although there is a record of a captive Orchard Oriole living almost seventeen years, the longest life span for a wild member of this species is nine years, seven months. For Bullock's Orioles, the longevity record is approximately eight years. The maximum recorded life span for a Baltimore Oriole is eleven years, seven months and for a Scott's Oriole is six years, five months. These are, of course, the records. We don't know how long the average member of any of these species survives, but it is probably much less. Life presents lots of challenges for these birds, as we'll discover.

ORIOLE PREDATORS

Having discussed at length what orioles eat, it seems only fair to consider what eats them. In fact, there are very few published records of observed predation on orioles. Most often, those who study the birds find evidence of predation without having observed the event itself or knowing what did the deed. Empty nests—with or without broken eggshells left behind—long before they should be, or nests missing one or more nestlings that had been there previously, usually indicate that a predator of some sort has struck. Parents that fail to return to a nest where they have been tending eggs or nestlings suggest the same. Identifying the guilty party is rare, however. A list of known oriole predators includes Ferruginous Pygmy-Owls, Cooper's Hawks, Western Scrub Jays, American Crows, Gopher Snakes, Common Grackles, Greater Roadrunners, Eastern and Western Screech-Owls, Red Squirrels, Gray Squirrels, Fox Squirrels, Blue Jays, Black-billed Magpies, and, of course, domestic cats. No doubt a few of you reading this book could add more culprits to this list.

Aggressive behavior on the part of orioles toward animals that could potentially kill them is often used to infer that these animals are predators. Most of the noted predators are vigorously mobbed by orioles as well as other birds. Mobbing involves flying at and sometimes hitting a target species repeatedly. Both male and female orioles engage in this behavior. Groups of birds—orioles joined by, or joining with, other types of birds—will often mob the offending individual together. Mobbing takes energy and could be risky (if the target strikes back), so it is good evidence that the animal being mobbed is a potential predator.

NEST DANGERS

The nests of Baltimore Orioles and Bullock's Orioles, usually attached to the tips of small branches, are fairly inaccessible to predators. Indeed, the annual nest success of these species is fairly high relative to that of many songbirds—over 80 percent in most carefully studied populations (closer to 50 percent is normal for many cup-nesting songbirds). As well, the huge nests of the Altimara Oriole are virtually impregnable. Nevertheless, tree-climbing snakes and small, brave squirrels have occasionally been observed gaining entry to these species' nests.

The nests of other North American orioles are less well-protected and thus seem to lose a higher proportion of eggs and nestlings to predators. In a study of Scott's Orioles in Texas, for example, only 54 percent of 124 nests successfully fledged any young at all. For this species, a number of predators were possible, although few were actually observed taking eggs or young. Many species of snakes are known to be climbers, for example, and to include birds in their diet. And rat snakes were found in the crowns of yucca trees in the area where the Scott's population was studied. Similarly, several species of mice, pack rats, the Ring-tailed Cat, and Spotted Skunks shared this habitat and thus were suspect. Although none were caught red-handed, clues such as pulled-down or damaged nests suggested their participation in the predation.

The female oriole gathers nesting material after choosing a nest site within her mate's territory. Nest-site selection is crucial to the survival of the birds—a well-placed nest is safer from the dangers of predation and bad weather.

CAT PROBLEMS

As far as published records go, cats have been implicated in the deaths of only a few orioles in a few places. The truth, however, is likely far different. Although the nests of some oriole species may be immune to cats, others are not, and the recently fledged young of all species are vulnerable to cats, as are adults foraging near the ground. Cats are, in fact, a serious problem for a great diversity of birds, as well as other wildlife species. In 2007, the American Veterinary Medical Association estimated that there were some 81 million pet cats in the United States, and the Cat Fanciers' Association, quoting an annual industry survey, notes that approximately 43 percent of these pets were allowed to roam outside. Neither of these figures includes feral cats, which are essentially always outside and, according to some estimates, might be even more abundant than pets. And neither figure includes cats in Canada, where they are considered at least partly to blame for the near extinction of species such as the Prothonotary Warbler, among others. It also doesn't include cats in the wintering ranges of orioles, in Mexico and Central America.

A range of studies have demonstrated that roaming cats cause serious problems. In England, during a five-month period, 964 cats killed 14,000 animals, 24 percent of which were birds (on average, each cat killed 16.7 birds). In Kansas, 83 percent of 41 studied cats killed birds regularly. Based on four years of their own data as well as data from other studies, researchers in Wisconsin estimated that rural cats kill at least 7.8 million birds a year in that state alone, and this did not include kills by urban or suburban cats. In California, a study compared two parks with grassland habitat, one of which had no cats and another in which 25 cats were fed daily. Over two years of the study, twice as many birds were seen in the park with no cats, and certain ground-nesting species were *never* seen in the park with the cats.

Clearly cats pose a number of problems. In addition to their depredation on birds, cats compete with native wild predators, such as owls, bobcats, and foxes. Unvaccinated cats can also transmit diseases to wild species; they are, in fact, suspected of having spread fatal feline diseases to native mountain lion (including the endangered Florida Panther) and bobcat populations. Many people love cats, of course—but they should be loved indoors, where they can enjoy the sight of orioles coming to feeders and raising their young in peace.

PARASITIC COWBIRDS

The family Icteridae includes several species of cowbirds, a group of birds that is most destructive to other species. Cowbirds are what is known as brood parasites—unwilling and probably unable to build their own nests, female cowbirds lay their eggs in the nests of a wide variety of other species, which become hosts to the young, often raising them at the expense of their own offspring. All but one of the cowbirds are in a single genus, *Molothrus,* and only two members of this genus breed in North America: the Brown-headed Cowbird and the Bronzed Cowbird. The Bronzed Cowbird has, in fact, only recently expanded its range northward from Central America and Mexico; it occurs only in the southern United States and thus affects mostly Scott's, Hooded, Altamira, and Audubon's Orioles. The Brown-headed Cowbird, on the other hand, is widespread throughout the United States and Canada and parasitizes Baltimore, Bullock's, Orchard, Scott's, and Hooded Orioles—in some areas quite heavily.

Because the Brown-headed Cowbird has had a significant impact on many North American breeding birds, it has been the focus of considerable study. The cowbird is often referred to as a "songbird chicken." Females keep laying and laying throughout a two- to three-month breeding season, producing as many as forty eggs. In about two-thirds of parasitized nests, the female cowbird adds insult to injury by removing one of the host eggs before laying its own. This behavior may reduce the chance of the host noticing the extra egg or help ensure that there is enough space in the nest for the cowbird egg to be incubated properly. Female cowbirds also lay their eggs strategically. They locate potential hosts by finding a perch in a location from which they have good visibility and watching the nest-building behavior of the intended victim. They typically lay their eggs before dawn, always during the egg-laying period of the host female. This ensures both that the host is likely to be away from her nest (birds spend little time actually in the nest when they are laying but have not yet begun incubating) and that the parasite egg will enjoy all the incubation time it needs to hatch. Cowbirds are in and out fast—they can lay an egg and be gone in as little as thirty seconds.

Brown-headed Cowbird eggs need less incubation time than those of most songbirds: only eleven to twelve days compared to twelve to fourteen days for most of their host species. As a result, cowbird young often hatch first, giving them an advantage over their foster siblings. In addition, cowbirds typically choose host species smaller than themselves.

Baltimore Oriole nests are less prone to cowbird parasitism than are those of other orioles, particularly the Orchard Oriole, which is generally the hardest hit.

Cowbird nestlings thus have a simple size advantage as well as a head start. Of the orioles, for example, the smallest species, the Orchard Oriole, seems to be the favorite cowbird host.

Many species, including all of the orioles, do recognize cowbirds and react aggressively, chasing them on sight. Some have even evolved the ability to detect the presence of parasite eggs: a few of the more than two hundred species that have been recorded as Brown-headed Cowbird hosts actually eject parasite eggs from their nests. The largest of the host species that do this are able to easily pick up the eggs and carry them out of their nests in a process called "grasp-ejection" (Altamira Orioles have been observed doing this with Bronzed Cowbird eggs). Baltimore and Bullock's Orioles are also egg ejectors, but they usually do so by puncturing the offending egg, breaking it, and then removing it piece by piece. Although this solves the parasite problem, it is a risky process, sometimes resulting in inadvertent damage to their own eggs. In fact, it's been calculated that for Bullock's Orioles, the cost of puncturing and ejecting parasite eggs is on average the death of 0.26 of their own eggs for each parasite egg ejected.

The impact of cowbird parasitism on orioles (as well as on other birds) varies with the species of the host, type of parasite, and location. It also seems to vary from year to year, perhaps with the density of nesting individuals, which may be related to various factors, including weather. Even different habitats in the same general area vary greatly in terms of the number of nests parasitized. Among the migrant orioles, the Orchard Oriole seems to be the hardest hit. In Illinois, a 1997 report noted that more than 90 percent of Orchard Oriole nests were parasitized (with an average of 2.2 cowbird eggs per nest) at Lake Shelbyville; in Shawnee National Forest (in the same state) less than 40 percent were parasitized, with an average of only 1 cowbird egg per nest.

Some populations of the Hooded Oriole are also heavily parasitized by Brown-headed Cowbirds. In suburban California, fifteen out of twenty-one nests (71.4 percent) contained eggs of this parasite. Baltimore and Bullock's Orioles, which eject the eggs of the parasite, are reported to be infrequently parasitized. This may be true—cowbirds may have learned to avoid these hosts since their success with them is so limited. Cowbirds do, however, lay eggs in the nests of many species that have never been successful in raising cowbird young and so the lack of reports of parasitism for these two orioles may be due to the fact that their nests tend to be less accessible to people than are those of Scott's, Orchard, and Hooded Orioles.

HOUSE FINCH PIRATES

Cowbirds (and a variety of other species) are called brood parasites because they leave their eggs in other birds' nests, relying on their hosts to care for their offspring. Another strategy employed by some types of birds is nest piracy—taking over nests built by other birds rather than building their own. At least one North American oriole suffers the effects of piracy by another species, in this case, the House Finch.

During a detailed study of Scott's Orioles in Texas, sixty-six of this species' nests were discovered while still under construction. Four of the nests failed to receive oriole eggs. In one case, the female that was building the nest disappeared and may have died. In the three other cases, however, House Finches laid eggs in the nest immediately after the female orioles had finished building (typically, orioles wait two or three days after nest completion before beginning to lay eggs). That these nests had been usurped rather than deserted was indicated by the fact that when the finch eggs were removed from one of these three, the oriole laid her own eggs (in her own nest) several days later. In the other two instances, the oriole pair remained in the immediate vicinity of their stolen homes, eventually building new nests nearby.

Even worse, House Finches in this area also stole nests in which orioles had already laid eggs. In one of the years of this study, a total of sixty-two nests in which orioles laid eggs were monitored over the breeding season. In three of these nests, entire clutches of undamaged oriole eggs were found buried beneath a new layer of lining material. On top of this lining a female House Finch sat, incubating its own clutch. The oriole eggs had been buried within a week of being laid, and in all three cases the orioles that had been robbed built new nests and laid new clutches nearby. These females had lost not only the energy put into construction of their first nests but also the even greater investment in a clutch of eggs.

BATTLES WITH COMPETITORS

Although all orioles react aggressively toward predators and parasites, they generally coexist peacefully with most other birds, defending their usually small nesting territories (usually just the area around the nest or nest tree) only against members of their own species. Where their ranges overlap, Bullock's and Baltimore Orioles usually chase each other around their nest sites, as do Bullock's and Hooded Orioles, but this type of behavior is not generally displayed toward other birds. Orchard Orioles, for example, are often found nesting in the same trees as Baltimore and Bullock's Orioles. And, despite occasional chases, Bullock's and Hooded Orioles can also be found in the same nesting area. When it comes to food, however, the gloves are taken off. Baltimore and Scott's Orioles drive away other nectar- or fruit-eating birds from particularly rich food sources: they have been observed chasing hummingbirds, warblers, tanagers, wrens, and other orioles. There is even a record of a male Baltimore Oriole killing a male Ruby-throated Hummingbird (in June in New Brunswick, Canada) that was foraging in a pea-tree where it was feeding.

AVIAN COMPANIONS

In contrast to their adversarial relationships with cowbirds and finches, and their aggressive interactions with species that compete for food and nesting spaces (interactions that are typical of all bird species), orioles seem to go out of their way to seek the company of some types of birds. There is considerable anecdotal evidence that orioles nest near various types of flycatchers. Some hypothesize that the presence of these birds may reduce the effects of predators and parasites on oriole nests. Orchard and Bullock's Orioles, for example, are often found nesting near Western Kingbirds. Altamira Orioles are often found near large flycatchers such as Kiskadees or Couch's Kingbirds. Orchard Oriole nests have been found a few yards from Eastern Kingbird nests, and, in a Kansas study area, the population of this oriole seemed to fluctuate with that of kingbirds.

There is also good evidence that where their ranges overlap, Bullock's Orioles prefer to nest near Yellow-billed Magpies. In fact, orioles nesting near magpies seem to suffer lower rates of predation than those nesting in the same type of habitat and in the same general area. It is thus thought that a preference for nesting near magpies has evolved in this species because of the protection they provide—magpies are a large species known for aggressive behavior toward the most common nest predators of the oriole: American Crows, Scrub Jays, and various species of hawks.

5

Oriole Song

How she can sing . . .
Make a lonely man happy, Baltimore Oriole
Come down from that bough

—Hoagy Carmichael

True singing requires the proper equipment, which is possessed by about four thousand of the roughly ten thousand living species of birds—including the orioles. The birds we think of as true "singers" are members of the large group referred to as the Passeriformes. This group, which includes about half of all birds, is further split into two subgroups: the oscines, referred to in lay terms as "songbirds," and the suboscines, which make up about a thousand species of flycatchers.

Numerous studies have shown that in many species, males sing more often than females. In some, song is the exclusive prerogative of males. Many female orioles *do* sing—in tropical species, their songs seem to be as full and as frequent as those of their mates. In the species that breed in temperate North America, however, female orioles sing simpler songs than males, and they do so less frequently.

Most people describe bird vocalizations as falling into two general categories: songs and calls. What differentiates them depends on how you define "song." Most of us probably think of songs as the longer, more musical, more complex types of vocalizations given by birds, whereas calls are shorter and simpler. That works—most orioles have a more-or-less species-typical song and a variety of shorter calls. In most members of the genus *Icterus*, the "standard" song associated with the species, although recognizable, varies at least somewhat among individuals. In addition, each bird has several slightly different versions of its song. This makes the job of describing and learning the song of each oriole species somewhat more difficult than for birds with simpler, less-variable vocalizations. This is, however, one of the features that make them so interesting.

Variability among songs arises from the way they are put together. Scientists who study avian vocalizations describe *song* as having four main levels of structure. First, there are *notes*—single, musical sounds. Two or more notes repeatedly sung together, and separated from each other by a brief period (perhaps only milliseconds) of no singing, form a *syllable*. When two or more syllables are strung together the result is a *phrase*. Finally, two or more phrases are then put together to form a *song*.

For an oriole, there usually aren't too many notes to keep track of in each song, or too many different songs per male. The typical adult male Baltimore Oriole sings seven to ten notes on average in a song that lasts about one-and-a-half seconds. Careful studies of the song of this species indicate that most males can be recognized by a characteristic song or set of songs. That is, an individual bird sings a certain set of notes, which it puts together in different combinations to make up variations of its personalized "theme" song. On average, most males had a repertoire of about six different, but similar, songs—each one made up of adding, subtracting, or changing the order of its set of notes. (This presents much less of a challenge for a human learning a Baltimore Oriole song than does the song of a Brown Thrasher; a male of this species may have a repertoire of more than a thousand different songs, made up of a large number of different notes.)

On average, Baltimore Oriole songs span a range of about 2 kilohertz (from 1.5 to 4 kHz), and most of the notes in the song range in frequency as well. That is, most of the notes can be described as showing frequency modulation—there are few are pure tones. Unlike people, birds can hear very short notes with very short intervals between them. They can thus detect a distinct series of notes that to us may seem like only one continuous sound. This increases the complexity of a song for an avian listener, allowing for the transmission of a more elaborate message.

The frequency with which a bird species sings and the extent to which its song shows frequency modulation depend at least in part on the habitat in which it lives. Various studies have suggested that longer notes sung at lower frequencies and with less modulation carry better in denser habitat, whereas open habitats favor higher frequency sounds, more frequency modulation, and shorter notes. This certainly fits with the North American orioles. In this group, the Audubon's Oriole frequents the densest habitats—breeding in cloud forests and tangled riverine thickets in southern Texas and Mexico—and it sings a series of long, drawn-out notes at a lower and more constant frequency than does its Baltimore cousin, which typically breeds in open parkland and in trees bordering creeks and fields.

Compared to songs, calls are much shorter, simpler vocalizations. Each species of bird has an array of calls that are used in different situations. Most are used to maintain contact between mates or between parents and offspring, indicate aggression toward trespassers or enemies, or warn of predators. Predator-warning calls are often designed to be difficult to locate, so the bird uttering them does not attract attention to itself. Other such calls, however, are given at a volume and frequency that actually attracts other birds to the caller—flock mates or even individuals of other species. Acting together, the alerted individuals can then mob a predator, distracting or annoying it until it leaves.

Oriole calls have not been carefully studied. As is true for other bird calls, they tend to vary less among the individuals in a particular oriole species, and there are some types of calls that seem to be similar even among different kinds of orioles. For example, orioles of various species have a distinctive "rattle" or "chatter" vocalization that they seem to give in aggressive situations. Other shorter, quieter vocalizations seem to help maintain contact between mates or between parents and mobile offspring. Nestlings have special calls that they give (sometimes quite loudly) to indicate hunger. Thus, each type of call has its own purpose or purposes—which brings us to the *why* of vocalization.

WHY DO ORIOLES SING?

Another way that songs are often distinguished from calls is based on their function. In this context, songs are described as vocalizations that are used to attract mates and/or defend territories, whereas calls are given in a variety of other contexts. Typically, then, songs are longer and more complex than calls—they are designed to send more complex messages. They also, therefore, vary more among species, as well as among the individuals in a species.

For a large number of species, various features of song (such as repertoire size) tend to "improve" with age and experience. In contrast, parasites and diseases seem to negatively affect some features, such as song rate. Thus, in a diverse array of birds, songs signal the quality of the singer—its health and status. As a consequence, depending on the species, males with faster, longer, more complex, or more varied songs get mated sooner and/or attract females of higher quality. Such males thus end up producing more offspring. And since the production of offspring— especially the production of more offspring than others of the same species—is the ultimate (albeit unconscious) goal of all organisms, song is obviously an important means to that end.

Orioles do not seem to play this game to excess, however, unlike mockingbirds or thrashers, in which males are pushed to attain repertoires consisting of hundreds or thousands of different song types. There is still pressure on male orioles to sing well. It is an essential skill when it comes to acquiring a territory and then a mate to occupy that territory. In Baltimore Orioles, males that are two or more years of age sing slightly longer songs than those in their first breeding season. And these older birds are more likely to acquire territories and mates than are younger Baltimore Orioles.

No one has yet distinguished which force—the need to deter other males from entering territories or the need to attract a mate—is more important in driving a male to sing or to have a larger repertoire. Both seem to be important, and as far as we know, male orioles sing the same songs for both purposes. Acquiring and defending a territory comes first, as this is a necessary requirement for attracting a female; for her, the quality of his real estate may be as important as the quality of the male himself. She will have to find a good nest site and at least some of the food for her young in this territory. The site will thus have to have a tree suitable for nesting, and enough shrubs and grasses to support an abundance of insects. Of course, the male himself is also a consideration. He will provide half the genes for her young, and they'd better be good. As well, he will be expected to help her care for these young—experience and good health will be assets in this regard.

It is thus worth a female's time to shop around. A male who sings less frequently or has a smaller repertoire may not measure up. In the North American oriole species that have been carefully studied, males somewhat outnumber females in the population and there are thus always some males who remain unmated each season. Song is probably an important indicator of which males will be losers (as is plumage color:

The quality of the song of the male oriole is an indicator as to the bird's health and status. Longer, more complex songs generally attract better-quality females.

first year males, which are duller in coloration and may sing less-complex songs, are less likely to get mates than are older conspecifics).

Why then would female orioles sing? To some extent, this may be simply a result of the fact that males and females share many genes. Thus, although certain traits are actually more useful for males, they may be exhibited to some extent by females as well, more or less as an artifact of this genetic correlation. This may be a major part of the reason.

These females do seem to use their singing ability, however. Once on a territory, a female is more likely than her mate to take on the job of chasing off other females. Both sexes can reduce the time and energy they spend in actual contact with intruders (or in actively chasing them off) by using their songs. The song of either sex says, "I'm healthy, I own this territory (or this mate), and I'm here looking out for it. Keep away!"

In resident tropical orioles, females seem to sing songs that are indistinguishable from those of their mates. This is fitting since, as you may recall, tropical orioles are monomorphic: males and females are both brightly colored. In these species, both sexes take a more-or-less equal role in defending territories. Although this is not known for certain, in the more densely settled tropical environments, there may be nonbreeding birds of both sexes—any of whom may be cruising for a mate and/or territory. The investment in a territory and a mate, which may be for life rather than for a few months, may be so great that males too may be somewhat choosey. A female's appearance and song may thus assist her in acquiring both of these prizes. Whether this is true or not, it certainly helps her take a major part in defending the territory against intruders. As is true for the migratory northern species, females seem to direct their aggressive behavior toward other females, and males stick mostly to fighting off other males.

Songs are also used, of course, for the purpose of identification. When you hear an oriole sing, you may be able to recognize the species of the bird giving the song. So will other listening orioles. They will also be able to determine the sex of the singer, its mating status, and, likely, its individual identity. An expert birder with extensive experience with a given population of birds may be able to do the same, but not as easily. This is particularly true for species like the Baltimore Oriole, in which song is known for being rather variable, with no two males singing exactly the same notes.

Being able to identify individuals—mates, offspring, competitors—is vital to a bird. Males of various species have been shown to distinguish the song of neighbors—who already have territories and thus are not threats—from those of strangers, who are searching for a territory and may need to be rebuffed. The ability to do this without having to see the birds and possibly get into a physical contest with them would provide considerable energy savings. Whether orioles can do this is not known for certain—neighboring male Baltimore Orioles, however, have been shown to share more notes and syllables than do any two random birds. This suggests that they may be able to recognize and pick up "tips" from each other, which would facilitate identification.

In contrast to songs, oriole calls seem less restricted to one or the other sex, since they serve more or less the same purpose for birds of both genders. Some calls, like the rattle or chatter, are used to indicate alarm or aggression, such as when a predator or a human approaches the nest or another oriole enters the territory. As will be described later, some calls seem to be given by only one oriole species, while others show features shared by several species.

WHEN DO ORIOLES SING?

As you have no doubt heard "the early bird gets the worm," and he was probably singing just before he got it. Virtually all species of birds sing most frequently very early in the morning. There may be several reasons for this. After a long night of being silent, those in the neighborhood may need a reminder about what territories are owned, and that the owner is still on guard. As well, songs seem to carry much better at dawn, when there is typically less wind and almost always less natural or man-made background noise. By some calculations, a song sung at dawn will carry twenty times better than one sung at noon. For the same reason, there is a second, less-intense bout of singing at dusk.

As well as singing more often in the early hours of the day, birds sing far more frequently in the early weeks of the breeding season. This is, of course, when song is most needed to claim a territory, defend it against other males, and attract a mate. For migratory birds that appear in the United States and Canada in April or May and take off to the south in the fall, the singing rate is particularly high in early spring. A study conducted in Michigan showed that shortly after they arrived during the second week of May, male Baltimore Orioles sang "almost incessantly" during the morning hours, often singing a long series of songs. Before the arrival of the female on his territory, the average duration between songs for one male in this study was 8.5 seconds, and he sang roughly six songs per minute. In contrast, after he had successfully attracted a mate, he reduced his rate of singing to about one song per minute, and the average interval between his songs increased to 37.5 seconds.

This pattern seems true of all migratory orioles: they sing with wild abandon upon arriving on the breeding grounds but become quieter after they acquire a mate and begin their duties of caring for young. They still sing during the rest of the breeding season, but at a much reduced rate (some researchers believe that they increase their singing rate slightly again in the fall). Orioles appear to sing at irregular intervals throughout the winter, with the rate increasing in frequency as the months wear on toward spring.

The increase and decrease in song rate is tied chiefly to testosterone. For most of the year, the gonads of both males and females are reduced in size, an adaptation that reduces body weight and thus the energy required to fly. As spring approaches and the time of daylight increases, the testes of males swell dramatically, increasing the production of both sperm and testosterone. These changes start to happen weeks before the breeding season begins, so that a male arrives on the breeding grounds in full song, pumped and ready to attract a male and defend a territory. One of the features of the brain cells in the song centers of these males is that they are sensitive to testosterone—stimulated by an increase in the amount of this hormone, at least some of these brain cells get larger, survive better, and increase in number. This leads to an overall increase in the size of the song centers as well as to improved connections among them. The result is more song and, in many species, more varied or complex songs. The fact that testosterone is a typically male hormone explains why males in many species sing more than females. Experiments in which females were provided with testosterone implants have shown that, at least in some species, female brains can respond to this hormone—females with more of it do sing more.

Of course, there are trade-offs. Although males with very high levels of testosterone may be irresistible to females, studies have shown that they tend to have shorter life spans. Testosterone increases activity levels, which may make individuals more visible to predators. It also increases aggression, which stresses body systems and makes birds more susceptible to disease. In addition, males with unusually high levels of circulating testosterone spend less time on parental care. Thus, once a male has acquired his territory and mate, his testes begin to shrink, producing less testosterone. The result is a reduction in the size of the song centers and a reduction in the frequency of song. The male's behavior patterns shift appropriately from those related to male attraction to those required for parental care.

Any bird singing a long, complex song will be an adult—it takes a while to learn how to perform this feat, at least for most singers. (This is, in fact, another way songs are typically differentiated from calls; according to many definitions, songs are learned, whereas calls are innate.) Song learning is a complex process. In general, it takes place in several stages, the lengths of which vary somewhat among species, among populations of the same species, and even among individuals in a population. In most birds, the first stage is what is often termed an acquisition or sensory period during which a very young bird hears the song of a tutor, usually its father. Most young birds seem to have an innate ability to hear and focus on the song of their own species almost exclusively. During this learning stage, the songs they hear are committed to memory and stored as a sort of template they will later use to match their own practice songs against. Following this stage, most species go through a silent period. Then, when the young are five to eight months old, they start to babble softly, much like a human infant. Referred to as subsong, this babbling eventually develops into something closer to the song of an adult.

Unfortunately, little is known about exactly how orioles learn to sing. The musicality and complexity of their songs indicate that they do learn at least some of their vocalizations. The exact timing of the stages, however, has not been studied. The fact that older male orioles sing more complex songs than do males in their first breeding season suggests that at least some learning can go on after the first year of life.

ORIOLE VOCALIZATIONS

This section offers an overview of the songs and calls of the most common North American orioles, with a general description of the song and calls made by each species as well as whatever details are known about variability, frequency range, and so on.

Baltimore Oriole

A number of authors have commented that the song of the Baltimore Oriole is easy to imitate but difficult to describe. The wide variety of descriptions that have been offered bear further testimony to this. "Whistled" is a term that is frequently used, as are "loud," "vigorous," "short," "clear," "pleasing," and "variable." Alvaro Jaramillo and Peter Burke, the authors

When it arrives at the nest with food, the male Baltimore Oriole often makes a quiet perk *call. Various calls are made in response to a variety of situations and stimuli.*

of a book on the family Icteridae, including the orioles, describe it as "a pleasant series of sweet, flutelike whistles." They note that "the song is short and abrupt, and most males sing a personalized version, with few sharing an identical song," although the frequency range of most males is similar, and all have the same overall tone.

One of the tricks used by bird-watchers to help them remember the song of a particular species is to make up a mnemonic—a "translation" of the song into words that mimic the phrasing or sound of the song. For birds with rather invariable songs, this works very well ("quick three beers" provides a perfect reminder of the song of an Olive-sided Fly-catcher, for example). The variable nature of a Baltimore Oriole's song, however, makes finding the perfect translation somewhat elusive. Common suggestions include "dearie, dearie," "peter, peter," or "look up here, peter, peter, peter."

Female Baltimore Orioles sing, but much less frequently than males. Their songs are similar to those of males, although perhaps shorter.

Like most other oriole species, Baltimores give a chatter call, which consists of a series—sometimes quite long—of repetitions of the same harsh note, sometimes described as sounding like a rattle. Unlike the song, which is heard mainly before pairing takes place, the chatter call is used regularly all through the nesting season, as well as on the wintering grounds.

Both male and female Baltimore Orioles also produce a sharp *chuck* call that seems to indicate alarm. It is repeated over and over at varying intervals during human intrusion into the territory, or if predators are nearby. (Interestingly, Baltimore, Orchard, and Bullock's Orioles can sometimes be found nesting in close proximity. When they do, birds of all three species respond to each other's chatters and *chuck* calls, even from a long distance away.)

A quieter *perk* call is also characteristic of the species. This seems to be used mainly to communicate between members of a pair. Females often utter this sound from the nest when incubating or brooding. It is often answered with the same call made by the male, who is usually sitting nearby. This *perk* call sometimes precedes a male's arrival at the nest with food for his young or mate.

One author, studying the Baltimore Oriole in an area where Bullock's Orioles as well as hybrids between the two species were found, described the use of a call he translated as *chip-weo*. Others believe this call is actually more characteristic of Bullock's Orioles, however. In both species, it is often uttered between songs in the spring, during territorial or mate attraction displays. Unlike song, it continues to be heard throughout the breeding season.

In addition to the calls so far described, territorial males often give low, harsh notes (which are not heard in other contexts) when chasing off intruding males of the same species.

Female Baltimore Orioles utter loud, harsh vocalizations, typically when they are being chased by males other than their mates. When they are being courted by their own males, on the other hand, they give a vocalization similar to the begging call of nestlings. They also give what has been described as a scream when chasing or striking predators or cowbirds (which, as nest parasites, are almost as dangerous as predators). Like many birds, including other orioles, females give a series of high-pitched twittering sounds during precopulatory displays. These are similar to the sounds uttered by fledglings trying to beg food from one or the other parent.

Although nestling Baltimore Orioles are quiet in the first week following hatching, they start to give increasingly loud and frequent begging calls as they get older. During the latter half of their time in the nest, they can be heard uttering a repetitive *dee-dee-dee-dee* cry, particularly when the parents approach with food. Just before fledging, the young vocalize regularly, even between feedings. After they leave the nest, they are quite noisy, uttering calls that sound more like *he-he-he* or *heck-heck-he* interspersed with loud twittering. One observer noted that these calls sounded much like an incessant "here we are, here we are." Although various authors have pointed out that these sounds may attract the attention of predators, their actual purpose is likely to help parents locate and feed hungry fledglings.

Bullock's Oriole

The song of the Bullock's Oriole is similar to that of the Baltimore Oriole but shorter and less variable. That is, each male seems to sing only a single, or perhaps a few very similar, songs. The song is difficult to translate: *cut cut cudut whee up chooup; kip, kit-tick, whew, wheet;* and *kip-y-ty-hoy-hoy* being some attempts. The last notes of some songs are usually clear and sharp, although they may trail off into a jumble. Some songs tend to start with harsh, scratchy notes. The songs of females are similar to those of males but harsher and less modulated. Both sexes sing frequently early in the nesting season and early in the day—females often from the ground, males usually only from trees.

Bullock's Orioles give a chatter call when distressed. A sharp single *skip* or *kleek* or *pheew* note seems to be used to maintain contact between the sexes. A soft *chuk* sound is also used, perhaps for the same purpose, although in other orioles this same sort of call seems to be heard more in situations in which the birds are disturbed. Nestlings and fledglings probably make the same sorts of begging calls made by Baltimore and Scott's Orioles.

Orchard Oriole

The song of the Orchard Oriole is often described as "lively," "loud," "musical," "whistled," and "varied" and is said to be reminiscent of an American Robin's, athough shorter. It is also similar to that of the Baltimore Oriole but generally higher in pitch and more rapid. It seems to be interspersed with more harsh notes than are heard from other orioles. Most songs appear to consist of a long series of notes (one study found an average of twelve notes per song, with a range of seven to nineteen), although short songs of a few notes are also given. The songs vary among male Orchard Orioles, have no easily describable pattern, and are hard to translate into words. Many seem to end with a downward slur. This, plus their general oriole-like quality, their rapidity, and the inclusion of harsh notes, makes it possible to distinguish songs of the Orchard Oriole from those given by Baltimore or Bullock's Orioles, which may be heard singing in the same area. Pete Dunne, in his *Essential Field Guide Companion*, describes Orchard Oriole songs as having a "distinct Tin Pan Alley quality. If Baltimore Oriole sings at the Met, Orchard croons at a saloon." As is true for Baltimore Orioles, the songs of older male Orchard Orioles seem to be slightly different from those of males in their first breeding season, indicating that at least some new learning can take place after sexual maturity. These differences are subtle, however. Female Orchard Orioles may sing occasionally; their songs are likely shorter and less complex.

Like other orioles, Orchard Orioles give a dry chatter in aggressive situations. They also make a *chuk* call that seems to be used when they are alarmed. This often seems to attract other birds, especially orioles, to assist in mobbing a predator. Females and young communicate with brief monotone whistles, especially when they are all foraging together late in the summer after the males have migrated southward. Males give a similar whistle earlier in the summer when feeding young.

Scott's Oriole

The song of the Scott's Oriole sounds to many like that of the Western Meadowlark or the Baltimore Oriole. In overall form, it is like that of the Baltimore, consisting of a rapid series of whistled notes, which vary considerably among individuals, but are still recognizable as typical of the species. Full songs usually consist of fifteen to twenty-five notes and last less than two seconds, but partial songs are also given. The comparison to the meadowlark is probably related not only to the fact that many of the notes are rapidly modulated in frequency (some rising and some falling) but also to its volume. The Scott's Oriole is often described as a particularly loud, frequent, and incessant singer. It is typically one of the first birds in an area to start singing each day, and it sings more throughout the day and the breeding season than is true of some other migratory orioles. It is also heard frequently singing on the wintering grounds. The song of females resembles that of males, although some authors describe it as simpler and softer, and others note that some females sing as loudly as males and their songs are equally complex, although less frequent. Mates often sing to each other when approaching or leaving the nest.

Calls made by the Scott's Oriole include a harsh, nasal *chuk* given when intruders or predators approach the nest. This is sometimes given singly, sometimes in rapid succession, forming a "scolding" vocalization. A softer, quieter, nasal *huit* sound is also given; it seems to be used when birds are disturbed but not as much as by a predator. It is often given by females when leaving the nest or by the male when approaching the nest to feed, so it may also be used as a contact call between mates. During precopulation displays, the female gives a rapid series of high-pitched, twittering calls, resembling the *huit,* while fluttering her wings.

Young Scott's Orioles are relatively quiet during their first week in the nest but then begin to give begging calls that can be heard from a distance when a parent approaches the nest with food. As is true for Baltimore Orioles, just before fledging, young Scott's vocalize regularly, even between parental visits. When soliciting food, fledglings give high-pitched twittering calls that are much like those given by females during precopulation displays.

Hooded Oriole

The vocalizations of the Hooded Oriole have not been well studied. Although the songs of this species are generally similar to those of other members of the genus *Icterus,* most observers describe them as being much less obvious—to humans at least. They are given at a low volume (thinner or fainter) and, compared with those of many other oriole species, are uttered from much-less-conspicuous perches. Furthermore, Hooded Orioles seem to sing rather infrequently, at least in some parts of their range. The terms "warbled," "whistled," "rapid," and "varied" are commonly used when describing the song of this species. Jaramillo and Burke comment that the song is "quick and abrupt. The individual notes are given rapidly and most lack the sweet whistled nature of many oriole notes; in contrast, they sound springy, nasal, and whiny." The length of the song varies widely. Whereas some songs last about one second, others are much longer. As is true of most species, females sing as well as males, although their songs are described as being less elaborate and less frequent.

Hooded Orioles give the typical oriole chatter call, although many describe it as weaker, fainter, or shorter than that of other members of the genus. They have also been heard uttering a sharp, metallic, or nasal-sounding *wheet* or *eek* call as well as a plaintive *whet* and a harsh *chuk* or *chek.* In general, the vocalizations of the species have been so little studied that the meaning of these calls is unknown.

6

Orioles Today and Tomorrow

Every year during the busiest part of the nesting season (June, in most of North America), a small army of volunteers—skilled in identification of birds by song as well as by sight—take to the roads to perform a ritual known as the North American Breeding Bird Survey (BBS). Beginning half an hour before local sunrise, census takers—often assisted by a driver and a data recorder—set off on a journey that may take four or five hours to complete. The same route is followed every year, with participants stopping every half mile to identify and count every bird they see or hear during a three-minute period. The stopping points are carefully mapped, and fifty stops are made along each 24.5-mile-long route, some four thousand of which are distributed throughout the continental United States and Canada. The result of all this work is a lot of data that is submitted either to the U.S. Geological Survey's Patuxent Wildlife Research Center in Maryland or the Canadian Wildlife Service's National Wildlife Research Centre in Ottawa. The information provides researchers with a clear picture of long-term trends in bird populations over wide geographical areas.

BBS data suggest that Hooded Orioles are increasing in North America overall, particularly in certain parts of their range. In California and elsewhere along the west coast, this may be due to increased planting of ornamental palms, which the species seems to favor for nesting. In several places, the bird's range seems to be extending northward: into Oregon, Washington, and Texas into the Guadalupe Mountains and on the Edwards Plateau. Hooded

Oriole populations have declined in the Lower Rio Grande Valley, however; once common there, they are now described as rare, probably due to the clearing of land for agriculture and the concomitant increase in cowbirds numbers.

Similarly, the BBS data indicate that the fortunes of Scott's Orioles seem to be on the rise in North America. Over the past thirty years, the bird's population increased significantly in Arizona, particularly in the Mexican Highlands and Sonoran Desert regions. It also increased significantly on the Edwards Plateau. More recently, however, it has decreased significantly in the southern California grasslands, an area where a variety of other species have also declined in numbers. Although it is not on any official list of species at risk, the Scott's Oriole is described by some as moderately threatened on both its wintering and breeding grounds, in large part because an estimated 11 to 25 percent of its preferred habitat has been lost. (The Scott's Oriole is famous, however, for its vagrancy—its tendency to be found far from its regular range in both summer and winter. It may therefore be better than some species at coping with habitat change.)

While the Orchard Oriole seems to very successful in some parts of its range, it is less so in others. In the past thirty years, it showed an annual increase of 10.6 percent in Canada, particularly as a result of its breeding activity in Manitoba and Ontario. In the latter province, it has extended its range considerably to the northeast as dense forests there became more open due to development and trees in urban parklands grew to maturity. Further increases, however, may be limited by a reduction of orchards and hedgerows (as well as the continued use of pesticides in the former habitats), the closure of forest canopy as opened forests mature, and the effects of cowbird parasitism. Orchard Oriole populations also increased in the northeast and central United States but have declined significantly in the southwest part of the species' range, particularly in Texas and Oklahoma. Much of this change is likely due to habitat alterations that affect the species either positively or negatively; increased cowbird parasitism also plays a role, as might conditions on the wintering grounds.

BBS data suggest slight but significant population reductions for the Bullock's Oriole in the United States, particularly in Texas and Oklahoma, where declines are particularly high in certain regions. The species does seem to be increasing annually in some parts of its range, including Idaho and the southern Rockies, but overall the losses outweigh these gains. In Canada, the species appears to have increased slightly when its abundance in 2007 is compared to what it was at the 1968 start of the BBS in western Canada. In the past twenty years, however, there has been an overall annual decline in the number of this species.

The Baltimore Oriole seems to be the worst off of the five migratory oriole species. BBS data indicate significant annual declines for both the United State and Canada, with steep decreases observed during recent decades: minus 0.8 percent annually in the United States; minus 3.4 percent annually in Canada (only three states or provinces out of the forty-four for which there is BBS data for this species show a significant annual increase: South Dakota, Tennessee, and West Virginia). Some or all of the usual culprits—habitat degradation, use of pesticides, parasitism by cowbirds, and poor conditions on the wintering grounds—are probably to blame for the declines.

Sufficient BBS data for reliable analysis of population trends exist only for species that are seen or heard regularly along a reasonably large number of census routes, and Altamira, Audubon's, and Spot-breasted Orioles do not meet this criterion. Other data, however, offer hints as to these species' population status. The species found in Texas appear to be more common farther south and are thus not considered endangered overall. In the United States, however, they appear to be struggling, mostly as a result of the combined effects of habitat alteration, cowbird parasitism, and severe winter weather in some years. Some estimates suggest that as much as 95 percent of the original native brushland forest favored by the Audubon's Oriole has been cleared for agriculture or other development. The species is, in fact, on the WatchList of the Audubon Society; its numbers have dramatically declined over the past fifty years in the Lower Rio Grande Valley, where it was once relatively common.

Although not as rare as Audubon's, the Altamira Oriole's future is also in question. Listed by the Texas Organization for Endangered Species as potentially threatened in the United States, its numbers have also declined in recent decades. Although it suffers less due to cowbird parasitism than does the Audubon's Oriole, the increased number of cowbirds in the state does pose a problem, as does habitat degradation.

In Florida, Spot-breasted Oriole numbers obviously increased after its accidental introduction. A sharp reduction occurred in the 1980s, however, after several severe freezes that damaged much of the vegetation on which the species depends. There is evidence that the species is recovering in some areas, but it now seems restricted to extreme southeast Florida.

Although none of the five migratory species of orioles are currently considered officially at risk, there are indications of population declines that could spell trouble if they continue. Much research has been focused on neotropical migrants in recent decades, indicating that more than a hundred species seem to be declining. What are some of the issues these birds face and what can we do about them?

DRINK SHADE-GROWN COFFEE

Millions of people in North America consume one, two, or more cups of coffee every day, most of which comes from Latin America. In 2005, world coffee production was estimated to be about thirteen billion pounds per year. Needless to say, that means there are a lot of coffee plants taking up soil and space in coffee-growing nations. Compared with many other agricultural activities, such as grazing cattle or planting corn, which usually require the clear-cutting of forests, coffee growing can be relatively environmentally friendly. Traditionally, coffee plants were grown under a canopy of shade trees in the company of a variety of other vegetation. In the early 1970s, however, fear of a disease known as coffee leaf rust caused many Latin American farmers to replace shade-loving varieties of coffee plants with newer ones that could grow in full sun. In addition to being resistant to the fungus, these plants also started producing beans earlier and produced a larger number of seeds per year.

Many have described this conversion as an environmental and social disaster. Sun coffee requires the copious use of chemical fertilizers, herbicides, and insecticides. It also requires the use of more machinery and thus fossil fuels. As monocultures without any other vegetation, sun-coffee plantations experience higher soil erosion and, in the estimate of some observers, employ fewer workers, leaving many without regular, or even seasonal, jobs. And from the standpoint of neotropical migrant birds, including orioles, they are sterile habitats in which it is impossible to find the food needed to survive the winter let alone build up sufficient reserves to travel north in the spring. Studies have shown that sun-coffee plantations support about 95 percent fewer bird species than shade-coffee plantations. A decline in Baltimore Oriole populations, as well as those of many other neotropical migrants, coincided with the conversion of a large number of coffee farms.

Fortunately, those concerned about these issues are attempting to ensure that the remaining shade farms continue to provide not only coffee but also valuable habitat for animals and income for workers. They are encouraging a move back to traditional methods of coffee farming. This all takes money, however—and we can help every time we buy coffee, either at the grocery store or a coffee shop. Look at the labels for brands that are certified "bird friendly" or "shade-grown" (remember that "certified organic" or "fair trade" coffee is not necessarily shade-grown). Such coffee can be more expensive, but most agree that it tastes better than sun coffee. And the oriole that returns to sing outside your window as you drink it will be your reward.

TURN OUT THE LIGHTS

Like many migrants, orioles do most of their migratory flying at night, an adaptation that increases their chances of survival. There are fewer predators around at night, and wind turbulence is lower, thereby reducing the amount of energy that must be expended to keep flying. The cooler temperatures of night also help birds regulate their body temperatures.

Finding the way at night is a challenge, but birds have a sophisticated navigational system that allows them to travel in the dark at speeds of up to thirty-five miles per hour for several hours without getting lost. Combining recognition of familiar landmarks, the positions of the moon and stars, and the directions of sunrise and sunset with an internal clock and a magnetic compass that can detect the earth's magnetic field, birds can navigate even on days or during nights when cloud cover obscures the sky. Their navigation prowess enables many individuals to return over thousands of miles to the same song post in the same tree they used the previous summer. Amazing!

The problem is that when this instinctive ability to navigate evolved, the world was a much darker place. Today, the sky "highways" used by migratory birds every night pass over numerous big and small cities, each of which emits a glow, creating the illusion of many sunrises on many horizons. This confuses many migrants, especially less-experienced younger ones, causing them to veer off course, losing precious time and energy or getting lost completely. On foggy or cloudy nights, many are attracted directly to these glows as they are to the stars they ordinarily use to migrate. Circling around the lighted structures, many become exhausted and drop to the ground, where they become easy prey for predators. Even more die hitting windows in a frantic attempt to escape.

Toronto lies below a major migratory flyway. In 1993, volunteers in Toronto were inspired to establish the Fatal Light Awareness Program (FLAP), after years of finding thousands of dead, injured, or trapped birds in spring and fall. FLAP members comb city streets before dawn to find birds they can save, taking them to large city parks, where they can recover. Perhaps more importantly, they work to raise awareness of the problems caused by night-time lighting, and they seek solutions. They encourage building managers and owners as well as workers and residents to turn off lights during migration. They have worked with city officials to design a "Lights Out Toronto" campaign and helped with the implementation of strategies for migratory bird protection through building design and use of less harmful lighting.

FLAP also challenged other cities, such as Chicago, to do the same. Today, members of an organization known as the Chicago Bird Collision Monitors perform many of the same functions as Toronto's FLAP. In 2003, with its own "Lights Out" campaign, Chicago became one of the first major U.S. cities to dim all lights during migration.

What is your city doing? Your workplace or residence? Could more be done?

PREVENT WINDOW STRIKES

Of course, the glass in tall buildings is not just deadly at night but also during the day; many of the birds that survive a night in the lighted city are killed the next morning when they fly into what looks like the sky or a tree but is really a pane of glass. Daniel Klem, Jr., of Muhlenberg College, who has studied this issue for years, estimates that at least a hundred million and perhaps as many as a billion birds die each year as a result of hitting windows.

Both reflective glass, which gives a mirrored image of sky and habitat, and transparent glass, which provides what seems like safe passageway to trees beyond, are equally problematic. Studies suggest that 50 to 90 percent of the birds that hit windows eventually die as a result of the collision. And approximately 25 percent of all bird species in North America—including orioles—have been documented hitting glass.

The solutions to this problem include some as simple as closing blinds or curtains whenever possible or at least when birds are most active (decals of falcons and so on do not cover enough glass to prevent most strikes; to provide a sufficiently visible deterrent, interference patterns must cover most of the glass surface and be separated by less than 2 inches horizontally and 4 inches vertically). The best solution is to use frosted or nonreflective tinted glass or a film coating that creates the same effect.

As well, bird feeders should be located at least 30 feet *or* no farther than 1 foot from windows; this will increase the likelihood that birds will recognize the window as part of a house and not fly toward it to escape a predator—or limit their momentum if they do.

FEWER AND BETTER TOWERS

In addition to cities, with their confusing lights and lethal panes of glass, birds encounter many other obstacles on their migratory journeys: emission, TV, and cell-phone towers; power lines; and wind turbines. And the tallest of these are often supported by numerous guylines. Such structures take their toll on bird populations. In one study between 1977 and 1990, it was discovered that 20,148 birds of 106 different species were killed at only *three* television towers in western New York.

There are things that can be done, however. Studies of migratory pathways can teach us to build turbines and towers where they will cause less damage. Red lights have been shown to be less confusing than white ones, and strobes less attractive than solid beams. As well, structures do not always have to be as tall as they are and can be built to require few guylines. Turbines could be turned off for a few hours during migration. And we could all conserve energy so that we need less of it to begin with.

MAKE MORE REST STOPS

Banding studies and other types of research seem to indicate that, for some species at least, mortality is higher during migration than during either the breeding or wintering seasons. For many, the journey north includes a nonstop flight across the Gulf of Mexico.

Well-stocked rest stops—what are termed "stopover sites"—along the way are absolutely critical if a bird is to make it to its final destination in good condition. They are especially important for birds, such as Bullock's Orioles, that have evolved to leave their breeding territories before they have molted in order to take advantage of rich feeding resources at stopover sites in the Southwest. Here they put on the fresh feathers they will need to be able to complete the long-distance journey to Mexico and Central America.

The disappearance or degradation of natural habitat is generally recognized as the greatest cause of bird population declines. Such degradation includes the fragmentation or outright destruction of nesting and wintering habitat as well as the loss of crucial stopover sites. Many of us could help by ensuring that our properties, small or large, welcome birds with native shrubs, trees, and smaller plants—a variety that will provide as many vertical layers as possible—as well as food that will sustain them on their way. Even small gardens can provide good stopover spots. And on a broader scale, we need to foster a culture of conservation, supporting national, state, and provincial, or local organizations that seek to maintain or increase natural habitat and do what we can to reduce our impact on that habitat.

AVOID PESTICIDES

We have so often heard about the hazards of chemical herbicides and pesticides that we may be almost tired of it. We phased out DDT long ago, you might be saying—surely what we are using now is less hazardous. Less hazardous, however, doesn't necessarily mean completely safe. If it kills insects, it is likely to affect organisms that eat insects, including birds. As well, as more forests are cleared for grazing and crops in Latin America, the use of agrochemicals is increasing rather than decreasing in that part of a migratory bird's world.

What can we do? The best course is to reduce or eliminate the use of pesticides and herbicides on our lawns and gardens. There are many natural alternatives (ladybugs, nematodes, and others) just waiting to be explored.

Reducing pesticides (and saving habitat and turning off lights) will save money as well as the lives of birds and other wildlife. Actions like these will help us ensure that we have orioles tomorrow, as well as today.

INDEX